I AM CREATIVE

BY
RUDE®

unleash YOUR CREATIVE SUPERPOWERS

AN INTRODUCTION TO CREATIVE CAREERS

LAURENCE KING

First published in the United States
in 2025 by Laurence King

ISBN: 978-1-51023-175-7

1 3 5 7 9 10 8 6 4 2

Printed in China

Laurence King
An imprint of
Hachette Children's Group
Part of Hodder and Stoughton
Carmelite House
50 Victoria Embankment
London EC4Y 0DZ

An Hachette UK Company
www.hachette.co.uk
www.hachettechildrens.co.uk
www.laurenceking.com

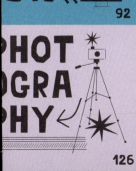
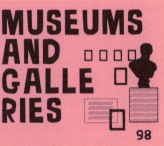

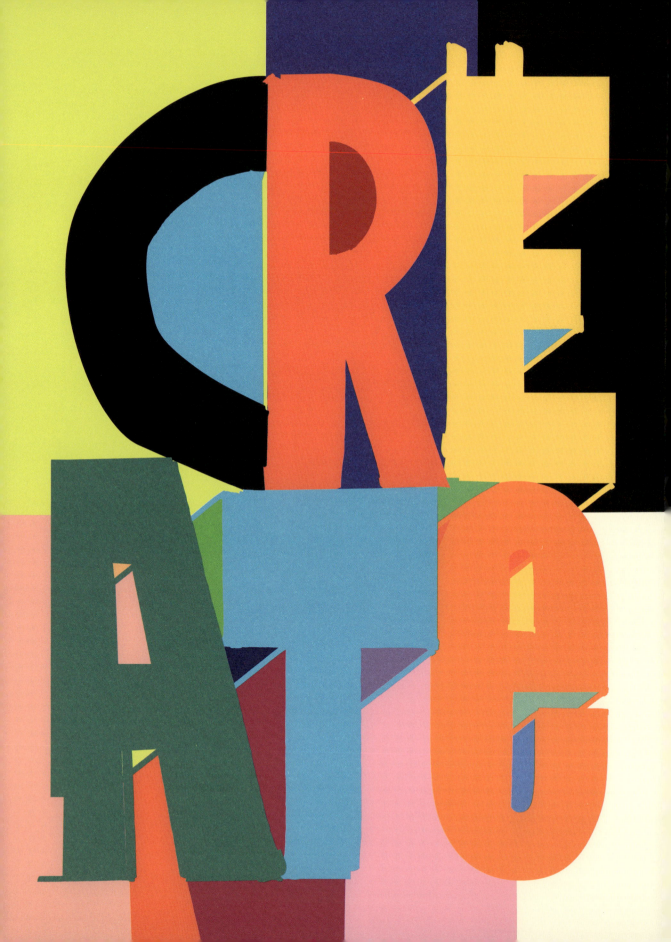

"LOGIC WILL GET YOU FROM A-B. IMAGINATION WILL TAKE YOU EVERYWHERE" Albert Einstein

Ever wondered who built your house or made your favorite movie? The chair you're sitting on, the shoes you're wearing, the music in your ears—they're all the result of amazing teams of creative professionals. These pages are packed with awesome careers, and we'll introduce you to some seriously cool people who make them happen.

Hi! We're Abi and Rupert. We run a company called Rude, where we draw, design, and create for a living. We're lucky enough to do what we love every single day, and we're here to show you how you can, too. We made this book to shine a light on incredible jobs you might not have heard of—jobs that could be your future! Sound like fun? Let's dive in!

Welcome to the World of Creatives

ARCHITECTURE

//

Architects create amazing places for people to live, work, and play, from giant stadiums to local playgrounds. They design the overall look of buildings and structures, think about the needs of people who will use them, and also make sure the buildings don't fall down!

skills

ART

Good architecture enhances a landscape, and the best architects have an eye for beauty and detail.

ENGINEERING

Architects have to think about how things are put together in order to make buildings serve different, complicated needs.

TEAMWORK

Many people are involved in construction projects: builders, heating specialists, interior designers, the list goes on. An architect must talk to them all!

PATIENCE

Creating any building can take a long time and have lots of moving parts, so you'll have to be willing to wait for the big reveal!

Architecture is a broad profession. Some architects design residential spaces for people to live in, others design commercial spaces for businesses or public spaces for everyone to enjoy. The construction industry produces masses of carbon emissions every day, so it's really important to try and find ways to use less energy. Especially in a climate crisis. So architects have a huge responsibility! Today, the biggest challenge for architects is finding clever ways to lower their impact on the environment.

TO BE A GREAT ARCHITECT, EXPLORE, EXPLORE, EXPLORE! OBSERVE THE WORLD AROUND YOU AND BEYOND. DRAW EVERY DAY. AND DEFINITELY LEARN TO WORK WITH OTHERS—ARCHITECTURE IS A TEAM EFFORT.

FOSTER + PARTNERS

ARCHITECT

Antoinette Nassopoulos-Erickson has designed airports all over the world, including in London, Mexico, Panama, and France. OK, and she has also made master plans of entire cities and the world's first ever Spaceport! She works for a studio named Foster + Partners in London, UK, whose specialty is creating sustainable designs.

The Virgin Galactic Spaceport in the New Mexico desert uses Earth as a part of its architecture. It is designed to look like a spaceship that has landed and has been hidden by the desert. The astronauts love it!

DID YOU GO TO COLLEGE?
I went to the University of Sydney in Australia, where I studied science for my first degree. After three years, I took a "year out" in which you have the chance to work or travel. Afterward, I came back and did my second degree, this time in Architecture. I later went on to do my Master's degree in Urban Design.

Hi, I'm Antoinette. When I was a kid, I thought I wanted to be a marine biologist. But then I started sketching undersea houses. My older sister bought me pencils and paper and told me that I should become an architect. Then, I moved to Australia and started thinking lots about fresh beginnings in a place where nature is intense and the cities are so new.

WHAT DO YOU THINK MAKES A GOOD ARCHITECT?

A good architect will look at a design challenge with an open mind and quickly work out the main goals. It helps to have a great imagination and the curiosity to keep exploring new ideas. Architects also need to be good at solving problems. Finally, you have to have a strong respect for nature, place, culture, and sustainability.

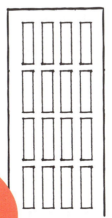

HOW DO YOU TURN A BUILDING FROM AN IDEA INTO REALITY?

Architects have to understand how to deliver their ideas. They have to understand how buildings are built, learn about different materials and how they work, and think about heating and cooling. You also have to know how to communicate and coordinate all the different specialists it takes to make a building.

Client

Whoever pays for a piece of work, whether it's a company asking for a new office space, a family asking for a new home, or a government asking for a new park.

Emissions

The amount of carbon that is released into the atmosphere. Building work creates a lot of emissions, as does keeping the space warm.

Blueprint

A plan for a building created by an architect that a construction team will follow.

ZAHA HADID

ARCHITECTURAL DESIGNER

Meet Jianfei

Jianfei Chu is an architectural designer based in the UK and China. He is part of the Zaha Hadid Computation and Design Research Group, and he uses visual effects (VFX) techniques from the gaming and film industry to change how buildings are seen and planned.

WHAT DOES YOUR AVERAGE DAY LOOK LIKE?

7 AM	Wake up, have a cup of coffee and breakfast.
8 AM	Stand on the balcony for awhile until my mind is fresh.
9 AM	Back to the desk. Organize important tasks and make a to-do list for colleagues and myself.
10 AM	Distribute tasks to group members. Have meetings with the group and explain the tasks.
1 PM	Lunch break.
2 PM	Creative tasks—design the architecture!
5 PM	Check in with group members, review the day's work.
6 PM	Dinner.
7 PM	Two hours of self-learning after dinner.

Jianfei developed an award-winning design concept called Architectural Configurator. This software allows many different people to participate in the process of designing a building – including those commissioning it and those who will be using it. His company used the concept to build a project in Honduras.

JIANFEI'S SOFTWARE SKILLS

To create his designs, Jianfei uses: **3D software** (Rhino, Maya, and Cinema4D); **2D software** (Photoshop and AutoCAD); **Animation software** (AfterEffects, Premiere, and Octane); & **Coding** (Grasshopper and C++).

Hi, I'm Jianfei. My father is a construction engineer, and my mother is a painter. When I was young, they often shared their proud achievements and joys from their work with me. Being exposed to both engineering and artistic knowledge from a young age meant that I grew up with a sensitivity and passion for design.

Engineering

The process of bringing an architectural design to life and making sure it works practically.

Archviz

A tool that uses computers to generate 3D architectural models.

WHAT DEGREES DO YOU HAVE?

I got my first architectural degree in China and a postgraduate degree from the Architectural Association in London. School provided a great working environment where I could access lots of learning resources. But throughout the entire learning process, I believe I was my own teacher, responsible for exploring the goals I wanted to achieve and acquiring the knowledge needed.

WHAT MAKES A GOOD ARCHITECTURAL DESIGNER?

Architecture requires a deep understanding of many areas, such as design, architectural theory, and computer software. To be a good architect, you must have a strong sense of curiosity and be able to quickly learn all aspects of the job. You need to identify your own area of expertise (for me, it's coming up with ideas and visual expression), and use that as a foundation to develop your unique skills.

THE ONLY CONSTANT IS CHANGE

Norman Foster

PLANTS AND ARCHITECTURE

Every building impacts the nature around it, and in big cities you`ll often see more gray than green. But urban designers today are bringing plants back into the conversation: They not only have to think about making their projects eco-friendly, but about how to bring real life into their designs with greenery.

This means thinking about how much light a space is getting, how to make sure the plants get water and how to drain it, and what types of plants grow better in different environments. For city-dwellers who can`t easily get to the forest, it`s a genius way to bring the forest to them!

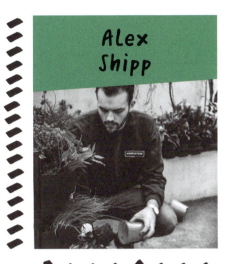

Alex Shipp

Alex Shipp is the Head of Design at Meristem Design, a company on a mission to "turn the gray green." They design green structures for local government and companies, taking over spaces that might not be used very well (like empty parking spaces or blank walls) and turning them into something that a whole community can enjoy.

Alex studied Industrial Design and Technology at Loughborough University in the UK, then completed an internship at a company that designed interiors for offices and hospitality spaces.

"I enjoy working with my hands," he says. "If a career in design was off the cards, I'd have gone into construction."

No two days are the same at Alex's job: Sometimes he's in the office or studio, some days he is on site watching construction happen, sometimes he is meeting with clients across the country. And now that more and more people recognize the benefits of plants in their spaces, business is truly blooming!

YOU SPEND A LOT OF YOUR LIFE AT WORK, SO IT IS KEY TO WORK FOR SOMETHING YOU FUNDAMENTALLY BELIEVE IN: THE FUTURE IS GREEN!

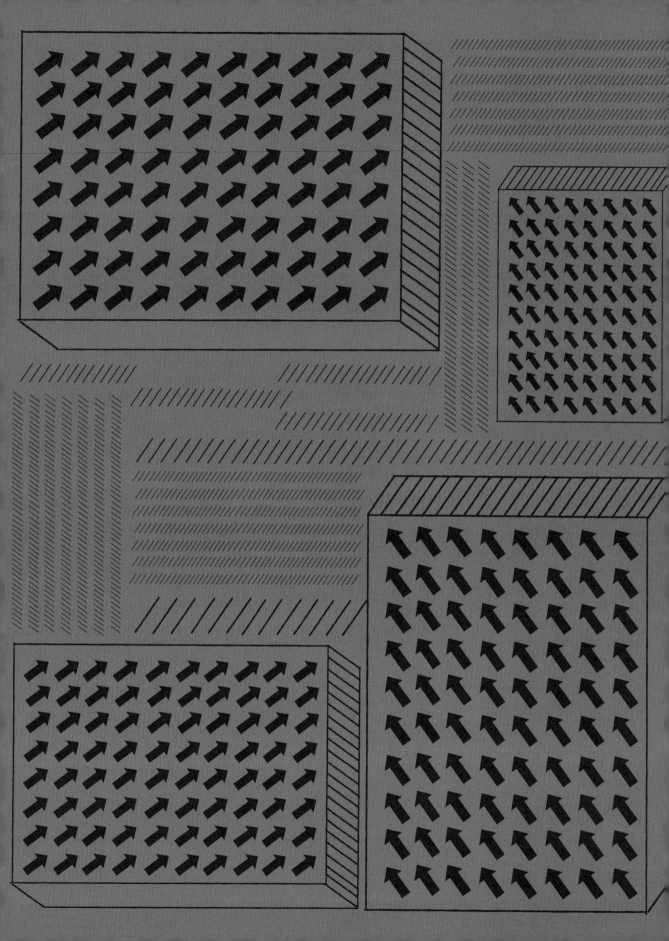

BRAND AND ADVERTISING

Ever seen an ad that made you laugh or think, "Wow, I want that!"? Advertising is a way for brands to show off what they do, or for organizations to promote important messages. You might see ads on billboards, on TikTok, or on the back of a cereal box.

skills

CRAZY IDEAS

Think outside the box! Great ads surprise you with unexpected twists, whether it's a clever turn of phrase or a live grizzly bear.

GRAPHICS

Graphics include a mix of fonts, drawings, and imagery used to give information. Interesting graphics are key to getting people's attention.

STORYTELLING

Good product advertising is all about telling the story of what your company makes and why it will make people's lives better.

HUMOR

Be funny! Ads are a great opportunity to express humor. People will remember if a product made them feel happy.

Advertisers have to be creative, coming up with catchy songs, heartwarming stories, surprising stunts, and more! Sometimes ads are hidden in places you least expect them: in a movie or inside a food package. Advertisers don't have long to make an impression, so the ad must be memorable.

Companies also need to think about creating visual signatures to be recognized quickly—this is where brand designers come in. Both advertisers and brand designers need to think about what people want and ways to communicate what a company is all about.

ACCEPT & PROCEED

CREATIVE ART DIRECTOR

Matt Jones is a Creative Director who has worked for Nike, NASA, and IBM. He uses design to solve problems for his clients, helping them tell the stories of their products in many engaging and exciting ways.

NIKE WAYFINDING

Accept & Proceed designed a store concept for Nike's House of Innovation in Shanghai. They wanted to highlight the amazing work of the Nike Sports Research Lab, through an interactive, motion-sensitive "Center Court" that gives you data about the footwear being tried on.

B-Corp

A company that meets the highest standards for being socially and environmentally responsible.

I remember how I felt seeing the cover of a compilation album I had designed for the rock band **The Flaming Lips**. We had photographed a pink plastic watering can from my garden, and the first time I saw it printed was on a huge billboard on the Tube (the London subway). That feeling was extraordinary.

LateNightTales
The Flaming Lips

Hi, I'm Matt. I have always enjoyed making things. In my teens, everyone was into big dance parties called raves, and my friends would collect rave flyers and cover their walls with them. I was being very particular about the ones I picked up and kept. I always tried to find the most exciting designs. In that way, for me, music was a great introduction to design.

WHAT INSPIRED YOU AS A KID?

It was through music that design found its way onto the streets into the hands of the everyday folk. I'd buy a record or a CD every week with my salary from part-time shelf-stacking; the sleeves were often fantastic in their own way. I remember putting a recording on and unpicking the sleeve design. So much more energy used to go into these objects.

Activation
A way that you make your brand known to people, whether through an ad campaign or a crazy stunt.

Campaign
A marketing plan for a product that happens over a period of time, in order to grab people's attention.

WHAT MAKES A GOOD DESIGNER?

Try not to overthink your design, or it loses its spirit. But don't under think, either! There's a big difference between simple and basic. Look for joyful contrasts in your composition. And keep tinkering. It's the journey to get there that's important— all the details created along the way are what form the bigger, final picture.

WHAT DID YOU STUDY AT SCHOOL?

I enjoyed art at school, and so I decided to study it at college, too. The art classes were way more fun than my other subjects, so I applied to art college. Despite one rejection, I eventually got into an art college—and it all paid off!

- BRAND AND ADVERTISING -

- CREATIVE ART DIRECTOR -

FIND YOUR VOICE. AND LET EVERYONE HEAR IT.

BBH

CEO

PEOPLE LOVE TALKING ABOUT THE GOOD OLD DAYS, CONSTANTLY. IT'S SO BORING! WE SHOULD LOOK TO THE FUTURE, IT'S WAY MORE FUN.

Meet Karen

Karen Martin is CEO for the London, UK, office of BBH (Bartle Bogle Hegarty), one of the biggest branding agencies in the world. Her role involves running every aspect of the company, including setting its overall vision, making decisions that protect the future of the company, and ensuring that the people working there are motivated to do their best creative work.

One of Karen's ads was a Tesco (a British grocery chain) campaign to promote adhesive bandages in multiple skin tones. Her work with Tesco focused on building trust and emphasizing good value.

Hi, I'm Karen. I've always loved ads and used to look forward to the ad breaks on TV. My mother is also a fan of advertising, so it was a regular conversation in our house. I did a marketing degree in Dublin, and the college was made up of art students and marketing students, like a mini agency.

Agency
A business that works with companies to create, plan, and handle their ad campaigns.

HOW DID YOU GET YOUR FIRST JOB?

When I finished college, my sister was working in recruitment. The agency they used to create all their ads were looking for new people, so she urged me to apply. I applied, got a job, and never looked back. Thanks, Michele!

EXPOSURE

CEO

Raoul Shah is the CEO of Exposure, a marketing and communications agency that makes brands culturally relevant. This means they target different audiences to help brands reach more people.

HuskMitNavn

Beyond the Streets was a graffiti and street art exhibition cocurated by Raoul, which took over all three floors of London's iconic **Saatchi Gallery**. The exhibition showed the impact of graffiti and street art around the world.

Janette Beckman.

Timothy Curtis

Hey, I'm Raoul. At school, I was quite a shy kid. I was friends with all these amazing people, but I always felt a little invisible. And to some degree, that suited me. What I do now feels like a reflection of that: I want to be behind all the great brands, but I also want to be a bit quieter than other companies out there. That way, people haven't already made up their minds about who they think you are, or what they think you will be able to do for them. That can be an opportunity.

SITTING DOWN AND HAVING AN ACTUAL CONVERSATION IN REAL LIFE IS VERY VALUABLE. YOU CAN ACHIEVE A LOT MORE.

HOW DID YOU START YOUR COMPANY?

I knew lots of people that worked in the media, in the fashion industry, in bars and clubs, and in the music industry.

I wanted to bring them together, so I started running club nights. I was approached by somebody who worked for a shoe company that wasn't doing well as a brand, and she said to me, "I want to ask people in your club to wear this shoe, to try and improve the company's image."

So, I said to her, "Come to the club with boxes of shoes!" We'd give the shoes away every Saturday night. Within about a year, I had six or seven companies that were all doing the same thing – giving me a small amount of money and a product to distribute among this network of people at the club nights.

Clearing
The process universities in the UK use to fill any spare places on their courses, after they have accepted the first batch of applicants.

WHAT DID YOU STUDY AT COLLEGE?

I left school with three A-levels (UK exam grades), and didn't get into a university. Instead, I went through the clearing system. The only course I could get onto was Textiles, Economics, and Management at UMIST in Manchester, UK. I had thought about trying to do something in the business studies area, but the textiles thing interested me, although I had no knowledge of it whatsoever. It was amazing to go to college, and afterward I eventually managed to get myself onto a training program at Pepe Jeans.

DAVE RAX

BRAND DESIGNER

Dave Rax helps organizations express themselves, from big tech companies like AirBnB and Netflix, to drink products like Fanta and BrewBike. He creates all kinds of adaptable visual tools for them, from logos and illustrations, to icons for their web pages.

Dave designed the new look for *Fanta*, which meant creating a new logo and font for them. He hand-designed a logo out of paper that would capture the bold, vibrant, and fruity taste of Fanta. You can find his designs all the way from your local supermarket to the beaches in Thailand!

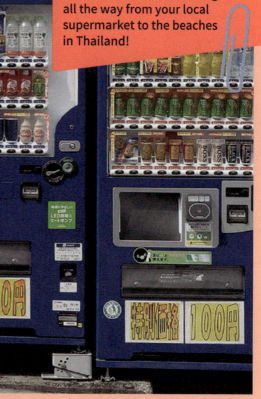

LOGO

A symbol or image that involves the name of a product, brand, or organization. It is designed in a specific, unique way that conveys what that company is about.

- BRAND AND ADVERTISING -

Hi, I'm Dave, and I design brands. As a kid, I loved music and skateboarding, and I would copy the designs from the bottom of my skateboards and favorite albums. No one told me that could be a job. Now I help design cool looks for huge brands that are known by millions of people around the world.

HOW DO YOU GET INTO A CREATIVE HEADSPACE?

To me, creativity is all about how I express myself. I feel creative when I do things like cooking or listening to music and finding bands I like. When I work, I always have music on in the background. It helps unlock my mind. Another thing that unlocks my mind is being in the ocean and surfing.

Identity

The ways that a brand expresses itself, like color palette, tone of voice, types of illustration, or animation style.

Your place to talk

HOW DID YOU GET STARTED?

Very early on in my career, I didn't really know all the different things that graphic design could do. The best way for me to tap into my curiosity was by sitting next to senior designers and essentially just absorbing what they were doing on their screens. That was the quickest way for me to learn, and it was how I worked out how to use all the software.

DON'T BE AFRAID TO FAIL. ONCE YOU GET RID OF THE PRESSURE, IT WILL FREE YOU UP TO BE MORE CREATIVE.

SAATCHI & SAATCHI

CREATIVE DIRECTOR

Franki Goodwin is the Chief Creative Officer at Saatchi & Saatchi, an advertising agency that works in 76 different countries around the world! She works with all kinds of different creatives to bring ads to life. Her company makes ads for organizations such as the British Heart Foundation, John Lewis stores, and the National Basketball Association in America.

Franki and her team partnered a German phone company with the band Gorillaz to create an immersive album launch using Augmented Reality (or AR). They used a green screen to bring the Gorillaz to life.

Out-of-Home

Any ads that appear outdoors: Ads on billboards, buses, and the subway escalator all fall into this category.

Hi, I'm Franki. At school, I used to draw self-portraits and Coke cans. Instead of junior and senior years, I did an Art Foundation course. I knew I wanted to study art at college, but I didn't want to paint or make pots. So, I studied Graphic Design and got really into typography and copywriting and film. Now I bring teams together to think of crazy, off-the-wall ideas that will get people's attention!

HOW DID YOU GET INTO THIS LINE OF WORK?

I was given a helping hand by **Design and Art Direction (D&AD)**, a company that helps young people enter the creative industries. To this day, it's an amazing place for support and to showcase work. From there, I had to start building a network of people I enjoyed working with.

CREATIVES ARE THE TAP DANCERS OF AN AGENCY—WE HAVE TO SELL THE IDEA WITH A PERFORMANCE!

Campaign

A big advertising push across lots of different placements—on your phone, on the train, on TV. People remember a message more if they see it a lot.

WHERE DO ADS AND FILMS OVERLAP?

When a movie launches, people need to know about it! Think about posters and previews, which help you get excited for something you're about to see. I've always been interested in extending the world of a film and created an agency called **Franki&Jonny** to do just that. How can you help the audience feel like they are immersing in the world of the movie? It's a great way to get people into theaters.

WHAT CAMPAIGN ARE YOU MOST PROUD OF?

For Deutsche Telecom—a very creative German phone company—we designed a game called *Sea Hero Quest* to help with dementia research. The data they got from people playing the game would have otherwise taken 176 centuries to collect! The campaign won nine Lion awards at Cannes, which is a festival for international creativity.

Portfolio

A selection of your best work that you can show people to help them understand how you think!

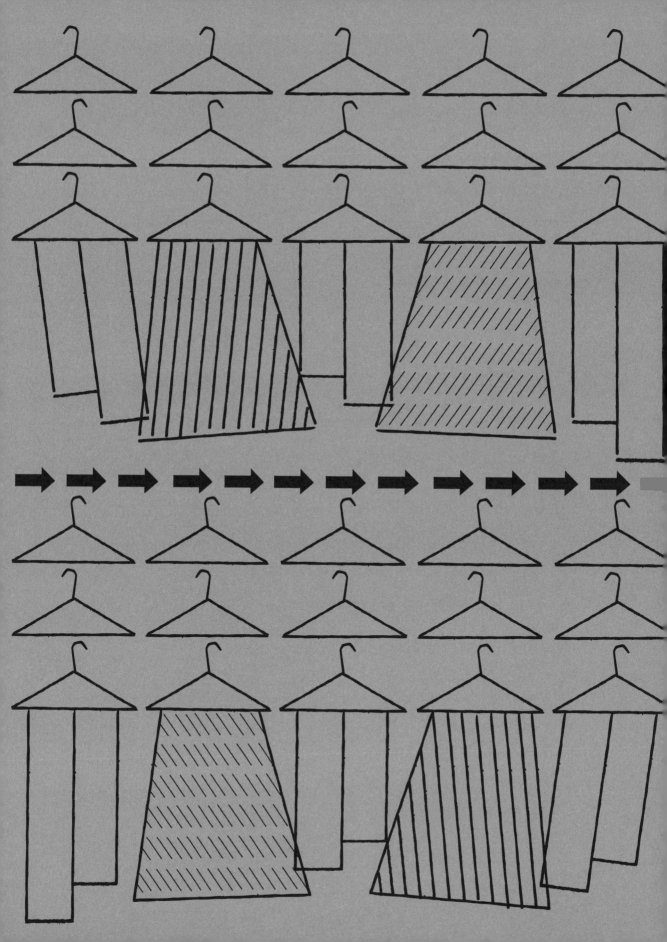

COSTUMES

Clothes that are designed for performance are called costumes, and they are often used to help create the sense of a character. A costume can tell you all sorts of things about someone: Where and when they come from, whether they are brave or shy, or rich or poor.

SKILLS

SEWING

When starting out, many costume designers make costumes by reworking old clothes and other materials from home.

SENSITIVITY

If you are designing clothes for someone else, you have to pay attention to what they need and how they feel in the costume.

ATTENTION TO DETAIL

Costumes are all about little details—zippers and buttons and hems that make something fit just right.

DRAWING

Before you make your costumes, you should sketch them on paper—that way you can find out any issues before you start cutting cloth!

Costume design is all about the drama. The most fun costumes are larger-than-life, expressive, and playful! In some types of performance, like drag and dance, the costume can become part of the performance itself, using tricks like tear-away skirts to create exciting reveals. A costume includes anything that a performer is going to wear, such as hats, hairpieces, wigs, shoes, and jewelry. Creating costumes for an entire production is a big job—you have to think about how they work together and play off of each other to tell each character's story.

WHEN YOU WORK FOR YOURSELF, YOU MUST BE SELF-MOTIVATED. NO ONE ELSE IS GOING TO DO YOUR WORK FOR YOU!

JILL MOLYNEUX

COSTUME, PROP, & PUPPET MAKER

Jill Molyneux makes props, costumes and sets for films, TV, theater, and events. This involves creating objects and clothing for stage or screen, from flying carpets to fire-breathing dragons. Along with directors and other designers, the props and costume maker brings the world of the story to life.

For a production of *Jack and the Beanstalk* at the Oxford Playhouse, Jill made a costume for a giant, which was worn by a man on stilts! The costume helped bring magic into the play.

Pantomime

A type of play that usually recreates a fairy tale as a slapstick comedy, and involves outlandish and colorful costumes.

Hi, I'm Jill. When I was little, I was always making a mess at home, using any materials I could find. Once I made a giant Christmas cake out of cardboard, wood, plaster, and lots of old buttons. Now I have my own company working with other freelance makers, and we've made all kinds of strange and wonderful things, including bear and cow costumes, giant babies, and puppets with animatronic eyes and mouths.

WHAT DEGREES DO YOU HAVE?

One of my high-school subjects was Fine Art, studying classic artists and learning how to paint and draw. I then did a year's art foundation course, but afterward decided I wasn't suited to college. Instead, I began a two-year diploma in Design Interpretation at the **Royal Central School of Speech and Drama** (UK), where I specialized in all aspects of theater, including costume, props, scenic painting, and construction.

WHAT MAKES A GOOD PROP MAKER?

A good prop maker will understand what needs to be made using the information supplied by the client, which could be a sketch or a drawing showing measurements, or simply a selection of reference images. They should use their knowledge of methods and materials to advise on the best construction process.

Animatronics
Puppets that combine human performance with mechanics.

KATRINA LINDSAY

SET AND COSTUME DESIGNER

Katrina designs sets and costumes for theater, ballet, opera, and film. She's worked with UK groups including the Royal Shakespeare Company, the National Theatre, and the Young Vic, to name a few! She has won two Tony awards and an Olivier award, and her work ranges from huge international productions like *Harry Potter and the Cursed Child* to smaller, critically acclaimed shows like *Small Island*.

Katrina won her first Tony award in 2008 for a Broadway play called *Les Liaisons Dangereuses*. On the night of the awards, she was provided with a chauffeur-driven limousine that was instructed to drive her wherever she wanted to go in New York. "Waiting to be interviewed by the press during the ceremony, I was looking over this city of skyscrapers and dreams and realizing that all the hard work for no money in basements in the earlier years was beginning to pay off."

Hello, I'm Katrina. I always knew I wanted to go to art school when leaving high school, but thought I would do fine art or ceramics. Then, in my first year, we did a two-week module on Theater Design, and I quickly realized that this was the area I wanted to study.

WHAT DOES IT TAKE TO BE A GOOD COSTUME DESIGNER?

You have to be able to enjoy delving into stories and worlds through research, creating visuals and communicating your ideas to others. You need to like being a team player. It's also important to understand all the other crafts and creative processes involved, in order to bring your design to life and take others on the journey with you. You have to be artistic, visual, and be able to draw and make things to communicate your ideas.

Bodice
A piece of clothing that covers the upper part of the body

WORK WITH PEOPLE YOUR AGE. THEY ARE THE NEXT SET OF PERFORMANCE MAKERS COMING THROUGH THE INDUSTRY, AND TOGETHER YOU CAN GIVE SHAPE TO THE FUTURE OF IT ALL.

WHAT'S THE BEST THING ABOUT BEING A COSTUME DESIGNER?

No two projects are ever the same. Plus, within any project, there are a variety of ways that the different costumes can be imagined and created. So it is never, ever boring. I get to work with a huge number of people that are so brilliantly skilled in their crafts. Luckily, my work has appeared worldwide, so I get to see amazing places and meet new people to collaborate with from a variety of cultures.

WIG CHAPEL

WIG MAKER

Jack Baxter makes fabulous wigs for performers. His first customers were friends and fellow London drag queens, but now his wigs have been used in theater, opera, and television productions all over the world. A wig maker uses a variety of materials, including human hair, synthetic hair, and animal hair.

Jack created this wig for drag performer Alexis Michelle, which she wore in a competition on *RuPaul's Drag Race*. The blue buns are designed to look like a crown of blueberries.

YOU NEED TO BE OBSESSED WITH EVERY LITTLE FACET OF YOUR WORK. IF YOU ARE PASSIONATE ABOUT IT, IT'LL MAKE ALL THE HARD WORK FEEL EASY.

Hi, I'm Jack. When I was a kid, I had lots of wigs in my dress-up box. I thought I might be a lawyer or a judge … probably so I could wear a wig (UK lawmakers wear old-fashioned wigs). I taught myself to make wigs by watching lots of YouTube videos. I had studied photography at school and college, so I started taking photos of the wigs and putting them on social media. And that's how people started to discover me.

Nape
The area at the back of your neck where the bottom of a wig fits against your head.

HOW LONG DOES IT TAKE TO STYLE A WIG?

From three to five hours. If there is a lot of detail, sometimes even two days of work. I work alone, so I always put a podcast or some music on in the background, something like Dalida's hits, Kylie Minogue, or Matt Corby.

Hair Weft
A set of hair strands that are mechanically woven onto the cap of the wig.

WHAT DEGREES DO YOU HAVE?

None! I have no formal qualifications for running a wig-styling business. I studied acting at college and in school. I was very good at art and photography. Everything I have learned has come from exploration—getting to understand my material and figuring out how to manipulate it and learn its limits.

WAS IT DIFFICULT TO GET INTO THIS LINE OF WORK?

I tried many different creative ventures and followed all sorts of artistic pursuits. Wig making was the one that finally stuck! It has been a lot of hard work, and being self-employed means you have to learn about business and keeping your money and finances safe.

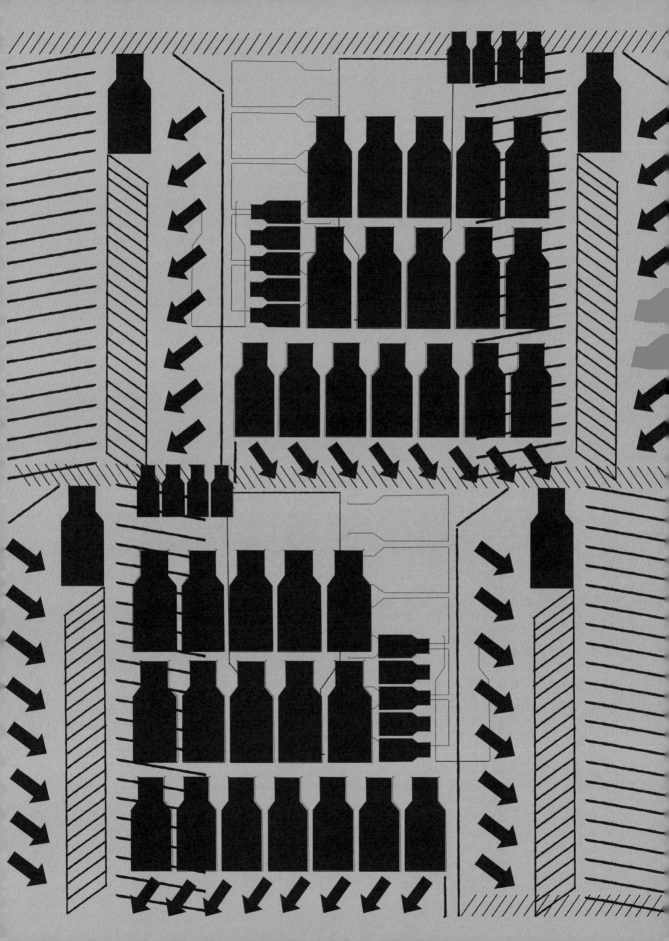

CRAFTS

Crafting is all about creating physical objects, usually using your hands, and requires the crafter to learn special skills or techniques. Jewelry, pottery, and all kinds of home decoration can be made by crafters.

skills

DETERMINATION

Learning a craft is tricky and requires practice, practice, practice!

FEEL

You should like working with your hands if you want to learn a craft. Most of them involve being very precise!

SELF-MOTIVATION

Crafters need to work hard and be creative to get their crafts in front of customers. You're your own boss!

PLAYFULNESS

Crafting is all about putting your own spin on a technique that may have existed for thousands of years.

People began crafting thousands of years ago to create solutions for everyday problems, such as making pottery to store their water or weaving baskets to carry their food. Crafting can feel like being a part of ancient traditions that connect us with our ancestors. But over time, crafting techniques have evolved to use modern tools and materials, and people have adapted their crafts to new trends in design and new uses.
For example, some advanced ceramics are now used as medical implants and microwave parts, while gemstones used in jewelry can now be grown in scientific laboratories!

- CRAFTS -

CERNAMIC

CERAMICIST

Meet Nam

Nam Tran owns his own ceramics studio in London, where he teaches classes and produces his own work. In 2017, he featured on *The Great Pottery Throwdown*. His mission is to inspire creativity through urban culture and promote a new era of ceramics.

This piece is called *Bahamut*, named after a giant dragon in the video game *Final Fantasy*. Nam was born in the year of the dragon, so the piece involves both childhood memories and the Chinese Zodiac.

TO BE A GOOD CERAMICIST, YOU HAVE TO ENJOY THE MISTAKES AS WELL AS THE RESULTS.

WHAT INSPIRES YOU?

My biggest inspiration is my memories. I'm always trying to remind myself of moments when life was different and fun. I think about my pieces as bookmarks, each of them reflecting a certain stage in my life. One of my exhibitions was called **No Ball Games**; I used to see these signs everywhere in London, and we would play ball games right under one of these signs!

Raku

A pottery technique from Japan, which involves making pottery with your hands instead of using a potter's wheel.

Hi, I'm Nam, and I make stuff with clay. I'm really inspired by toys and video games, and a lot of what I make is inspired by memories of my childhood. I was born in Vietnam and moved to the UK as a young person. My mom always used to give us stuff to play with and make things from—if we didn't have clay, she'd give us balls of dough.

WHAT DEGREES DO YOU HAVE?

I studied at the school of art at **Central Saint Martins** and the **Royal College of Art** in the UK. I first took an Art Foundation course, which allowed me to experiment with different types of art, but I found ceramics the most exciting because it allowed me to quickly translate ideas into a 3D form.

IF YOU DIDN'T MAKE CERAMICS, WHAT JOB WOULD YOU DO?

I would probably be a plumber. I just love working with my hands!

Kiln

A very hot oven used to harden clay into ceramics, tiles, or bricks. The earliest known kiln was in 6,000 BCE !

MOLTEN 1090

GLASSBLOWER

Laura Smith is a cofounder, creative director, and glassblower at Molten 1090, and she's also the founder of Laura Elizabeth Glass. Born and raised on the island of Bermuda, her work often explores the natural world such as volcanoes, the ocean, and the impact of storms. She has created one-of-a-kind pieces for private clients, fancy hotels, and cruise ships.

Laura opened her own studio in East London with her sister, Emily, who handles the business side of things. Having her own glass studio allows her to be even more creative and experimental with her craft.

WHAT DO YOU THINK ABOUT WHEN YOU'RE DESIGNING GLASS?

I love beautiful things, and I'm not interested in just making "the thing." I'm thinking of the person using the piece and whether it has a place in the world. I don't want to create pieces that sit in a cupboard or are locked away in a display case.

Hi, I'm Laura, and I make wonderful things with glass. Using my hands to create things has always felt very natural. I saw glassblowing for the first time at Dockyard Glassworks, a glassblowing studio in Bermuda, and I knew right away that I wanted to make glass. Then I enrolled on a glassblowing course on the Venetian island of Murano, in Italy, where I received my first ever lesson. I've never looked back since!

WHAT DOES AN AVERAGE DAY LOOK LIKE FOR YOU?

It's an early start, usually around 6 a.m. or 7 a.m., when I fire up the furnace to melt the glass in preparation for a full day of glassblowing. I follow a strict step-by-step process to ensure that the glass is melted properly. Then the fun begins, and I'll work with an assistant to blow glass pieces for about seven hours before putting the final piece in the kiln.

Blowing

The process of inflating molten glass on the end of a blowpipe. Air is blown through the pipe to inflate the glass into shapes.

Reheating

When you raise the temperature of the glass object you are working on, in order to keep shaping it.

A SKILLED GLASSBLOWER CAN FIND CALM IN THE HOT SHOP. BEING ADAPTABLE IN HIGH PRESSURE ENVIRONMENTS IS A PLUS.

IS IT HARD TO BECOME A GLASSBLOWER?

Yes. Access to studios is limited, and costs are high. When I started, there were only a few glassblowing studios in London, so it wasn't accessible, and it was hard to make a network. I'd recommend that artists work as part of a collective of creatives, so you can pool resources for a shared studio.

PRINT CLUB LONDON

PRINTMAKER

Meet Rose

Rose Stallard is the creative director and cofounder of Print Club London. She splits her time between commissions that she gets through Print Club and her own projects. Everything Rose does is injected with a little hint of rock 'n' roll.

ANY TIPS FOR ASPIRING ILLUSTRATORS/ PRINTMAKERS?

Keep making art; try out new things; get a studio space with other artists. Talk about your work with each other; go to shows; get your artwork out there.

PRINT CLUB LONDON
LIMITED EDITION SCREENPRINTS

Print Club's first event was Blisters—a screen print show for emerging and established artists. Alongside colleagues, Rose has worked to make Print Club one of the best studios for printmaking in the UK.

Creative Director

The person who is responsible for inventing the strategic vision for a campaign and bringing it to life.

Hi, I'm Rose. Both my parents came from creative backgrounds—my mom worked in fashion, and my dad was an architect. I don't think there's really been a time when I haven't been making stuff. After art school, I would be painting backdrops for parties, screenprinting T-shirts out of my bedroom, and making flyers for bands. Then I got a solo show at Dazed Gallery, found an illustration agent, and started Print Club London.

WAS IT HARD TO GET INTO THIS LINE OF WORK?

I think you just have to want to do it and constantly push yourself to make new work for people to see. It was a bit different when I started out, since you didn't have things like Instagram, so you had to send people your work in order to get on their radar.

Screenprinting
The process of pressing ink through a stenciled mesh screen to create a printed design.

THE BUSINESS SIDE OF BEING AN ARTIST IS AS IMPORTANT AS MAKING. I THINK THAT IT'S SOMETHING ALL ARTISTS SHOULD CONSIDER WHEN STARTING OUT.

DIGITAL

Today, digital tools are used to create art that could only be imagined in physical space. Software can create distinctive shapes, patterns, and textures that look totally different to other visual art processes. Digital designers also create the screens you interact with every day, helping you to navigate your online journey.

SKILLS

TARGET

Digital designers need to think about how different people will understand and interact with their designs.

PRECISION

Working with the tiniest pixels is a big part of being a digital designer, in order to communicate what can be done on a particular page.

ANALYSIS

Because apps and web pages often have analytics built in, digital designers get lots of data about how people are interacting with their work.

VISUAL LANGUAGE

Screens can communicate without words. Icons and logos can save space and help people who can't read or who speak different languages.

Think of your favorite app on your phone or tablet. When you open it up, what do you see? How do you know what to click? How do the colors work to indicate what options are available to you? All of these were choices that were made by a Visual Experience (VX) designer (or team of). In the tech world, designers are always thinking about how to make your journey as smooth and simple as possible, while also incorporating elements of playfulness and joy, as well as the identity of the brand or product that they are working with.

UX and UI

The User Interface (UI) is like the controllers you use to play the game, and the User Experience (UX) is how fun and easy it is to play. So, UI is how things look and UX is how things feel when you're playing your game.

STUDIO BLUP

Meet Dines

Dines is the founder of the award-winning Studio BLUP, a creative company based in London. They make futuristic digital art that has been used on the covers of music albums and magazines, and as advertisements for different products, including phones, sneakers, and TV channels.

WHAT MAKES A GOOD CREATIVE?

Creativity isn't just about inspiration; it's also about education. Asking questions, being eager to learn, and seeking guidance from industry leaders is vital. I've always believed in the power of mentorship and in the value of surrounding oneself with those who have walked the path before you.

Studio BLUP worked with Metallica and the record label **EMI** to celebrate the release of Metallica's eleventh studio album: *72 Seasons*. BLUP built a 3D model of objects from the album cover to create an immersive experience on four-story, 360-degree screens in the heart of London.

Hey, I'm Dines. Growing up, my surroundings were filled with art. My parents always championed self-expression, encouraging me to pick up a pencil or brush and just let my imagination run wild. Every scribble or drawing I made was met with admiration, giving me a buzz that's hard to describe. I remember venturing into the digital realm on my uncle's old Atari computer, meticulously crafting Pokémon and Anime characters pixel by pixel.

HOW DID YOU FORM YOUR STUDIO?

Instead of waiting for opportunities to knock, I chose to be proactive. I aspired not only to shape my own destiny, but also to be audacious enough to launch a brand that mirrored my values. The name "BLUP" came from my favorite letters that I always used to sketch, and it symbolizes simplicity and distinctiveness —two elements I wanted to infuse into my work. Then my dear friend Alex hopped aboard, shouldering the operational aspects of Studio BLUP.

WHAT DID YOU STUDY AT SCHOOL?

I achieved an A for all my art exams in high school. But it wasn't just traditional art subjects that captured my imagination: courses like Design Technology and Drama became outlets for my creativity. These subjects not only amplified my passion, but bolstered my confidence, pushing the boundaries of what I believed I could achieve.

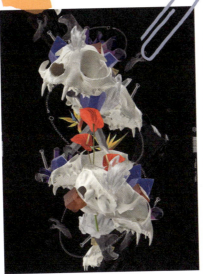

IN A RAPIDLY CHANGING WORLD, A GOOD DESIGNER NEEDS THE AGILITY TO PIVOT, EVOLVE, AND EMBRACE NEW TECHNIQUES, TOOLS, AND TRENDS. IT'S ABOUT CREATING DESIGNS THAT RESONATE TODAY AND REMAIN RELEVANT TOMORROW.

Augmented Reality (AR)

A type of technology that allows digital images and information to be projected onto the physical environment.

ダインズ

FEAR OF GOD

FEAR OF GOD

- DIGITAL -

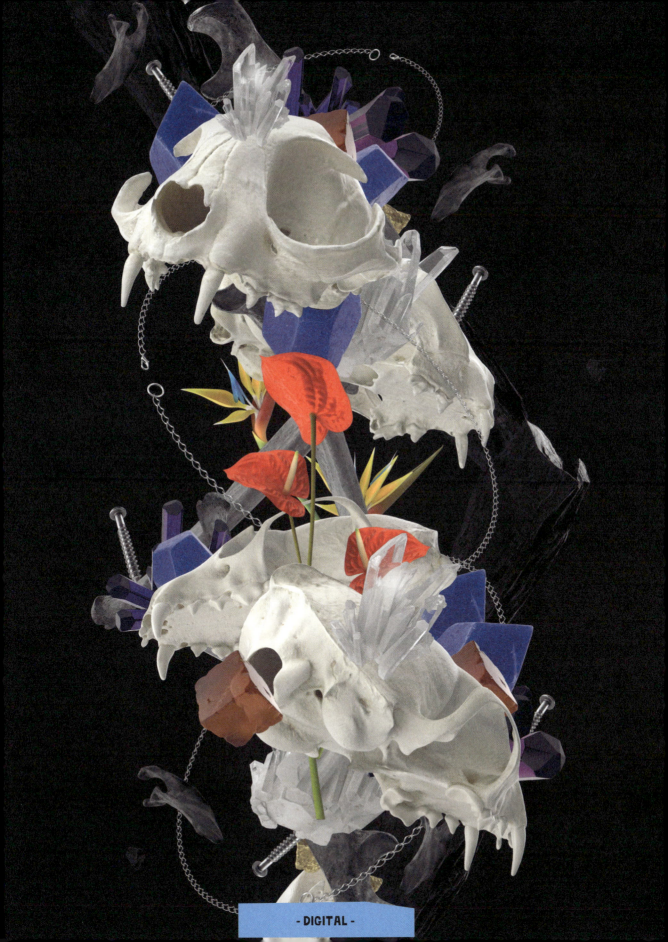

- DIGITAL -

USTWO

DIGITAL PRODUCT DESIGNER

Meet Kodj

Kodj Glover is a digital product designer at a studio called ustwo, making award-winning digital products. ustwo works with companies to make their user experiences playful and inclusive. Kodj also works with "Where are the Black Designers?," an organization that supports Black creatives worldwide.

One project that Kodj worked on at ustwo was with **The Body Coach**, a fitness company that started off as just one personal trainer working in a park. Kodj helped them build an app used by thousands of people to create personal workouts and get healthier!

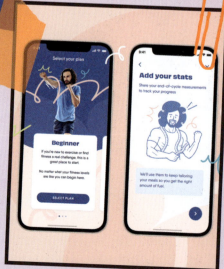

SPONGE UP THE GAME. THINK ABOUT WHAT MAKES A DIGITAL PRODUCT "GOOD" IN YOUR EYES. KEEP YOUR INTERESTS WIDE, AND DO THINGS OUTSIDE OF DESIGN!

Hey, I'm Kodj. For years, I was attracted to design and aesthetics. I combined this with my interest in music in the early blog era, and I got really into DIY mixtapes and mixtape artwork. This really revealed my aptitude for design and for working with artists on a collective vision.

Feature
Any aspect of a design that performs a specific, meaningful function.

WAS IT DIFFICULT TO GET INTO THIS LINE OF WORK?

In some ways, yes. Having no real understanding of the working digital design industry and no official design experience, it was a little challenging once I identified that this was what I wanted to do. But I think my passion to learn, and my diverse range of interests outside of design, meant that I could bring a refreshing perspective to the industry.

Wireframe
A first digital outline of a user interface, usually in black and white, that shows the basic layout of a design.

WHAT'S YOUR PROUDEST ACHIEVEMENT?

Being able to support youth programs like FlipSide that focus on empowering young people from marginalized backgrounds, and giving them the skills to get into digital design. Seeing some of the young people go on to secure jobs and even work beside them has been a massive highlight.

WHAT MAKES A GOOD DIGITAL PRODUCT DESIGNER?

Being unafraid to share your ideas or to work with other people. You need to really push to make an idea work, so that it can appeal to a mass audience and can successfully influence or educate those who use it.

FASHION

Fashion is the way people express themselves through clothing, accessories, and styles. It's like choosing your favorite colors, patterns, or designs to show the world who you are or how you're feeling. Fashion changes over time, with new trends coming in and old ones coming back. Fashion is like art that you can make and wear. Everyone has their own style, and that's what makes fashion fun—it's all about being creative and unique!

skills

SEWING

Being able to use a sewing machine or a needle and thread to create your own clothes is an essential skill for a fashionista.

DRAWING

Fashion designers need to be able to express their ideas through drawing and imagine their clothes on people of different shapes and sizes.

STYLING

Creating a complete outfit means understanding which colors and shapes go well together. Don't forget the accessories!

PRINTMAKING

Many fashion designers create their own prints for their clothing to create unique and memorable looks.

Think about the clothes that you are wearing right now. How does the color or pattern make you feel? Is the fabric soft or stiff, casual, or formal? Could you wear your outfit to a party, or is it more of an at-home outfit?

All of these are questions that people in the fashion industry think about when they are creating clothes. Whether it's the uniforms for your favorite sports team, or your best swimsuit, everything you wear has been designed for you by someone in the fashion industry.

HARRY WHITHAM

COSTUME DESIGNER & MAKER

Harry Whitham works with people to make the outfits of their dreams. Many of his costumes are worn by famous drag queens, and his work features regularly on the British version of hit TV show *RuPaul's Drag Race*. One of his pieces has been acquired by the Victoria & Albert museum's permanent collection in Glasgow, Scotland.

This coat dress was worn by drag queen Krystal Versace on *RuPaul's Drag Race* in the UK. The coat is decorated with what Harry calls "Wearable Fancy Patches," which are like artwork attached to an outfit!

Hi, I'm Harry. When I was a kid, I drew constantly, and I was always, always drawing people—mostly women. I used to come up with stories about different characters and ended up with sketchbooks full of fantastical women in amazing clothes. My mom worked in a doctor's office, and all my paper when I was younger was the back of old files that she'd bring home from work. She was constantly supplying me with free materials.

Drag Performance

A form of entertainment that celebrates gay culture that involves dress-up, lip-syncing or singing, and dancing.

WHAT DID YOUR FAMILY THINK OF YOU WORKING IN FASHION?

When I was sixteen, I applied to **London College of Fashion** to do a year-long course. My mom let me apply because she didn't think I would get in. And then I did, and she was like, "Oh great, now I have to let him move to London!" So she took me down from Shetland, Scotland, two months after I turned seventeen. When I left her at the train station in London, she basically had a panic attack.

WHERE DID YOU LEARN TO SEW?

My mom taught me how to do basic sewing when I was a child. But once I started designing fancy clothes, I realized I couldn't afford to get anyone to make them, so I better improve my sewing skills and do them myself! I got a lot of practice designing for my friends, some of whom were drag queens and needed lots of costumes.

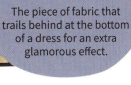

Train

The piece of fabric that trails behind at the bottom of a dress for an extra glamorous effect.

WHAT IS YOUR PROCESS LIKE?

People come to me with an idea they have about their outfit, and then I go away and do a sketch on my iPad. If there needs to be any amendments, whether it's color changes or lengths of trains or different materials, I can change it really quickly on the iPad.

1

2

Once we've agreed on that sketch, then we agree on the fee (which is very important when it's your business).

3

I then either work with sewers, or I work by myself. I'll cut the patterns, find the fabrics, and sew it together. Then I will have the person put it on, and I make small changes.

IT'S NOT ONLY OKAY TO BE QUEER AND NOT FIT THE STATUS QUO, IT'S ACTUALLY CELEBRATED. AND YOU CAN HAVE A REALLY FULFILLING, CREATIVE JOB THAT'LL PAY YOUR BILLS.

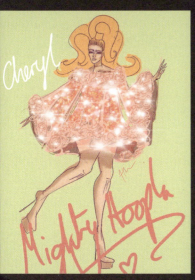

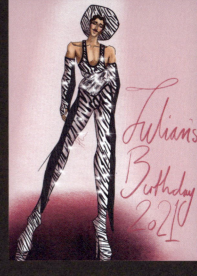

FASHION AND GRAPHICS

Fashion is all about making statements, and graphic designers who work in fashion use every tool available to do just that. Graphic design in fashion involves creating patterns and prints for clothing, and using illustrations and typography to make pieces stand out. Graphics on clothing can communicate humor, status, or helpful information. They can make an outfit loud or quiet, formal or informal.

Think about band T-shirts, employee uniforms, or designer brand logos. Repeating a bold pattern can create punchy impact, and using a small typeface can draw people in closer. Clothing is a signal for how other people should interact with you—and graphic fashion designers help your outfits do the talking for you.

Asya Smailbegovic

Asya started sketching her own printed shirt designs when she was in primary school. When she was older, she started customizing her clothes and wearing them out. Soon, her friends gave her their clothes to customize, too! She did a foundation course in Art and Design, followed by a degree in Graphic Design, which taught her to focus on the background and storytelling behind each project. Through work placements and internships, she built a portfolio, which helped her show off her work.

Now Asya works at **Nike** where she designs the uniforms for major women's soccer teams. Around the world, more and more fans are getting excited about the women's game, with a record turnout at the 2023 World Cup. And with designers like Asya at the forefront, Nike is making sure the world's top female players look second to none!

MY STYLE?
VIBRANT, FUN,
LOUD & ENERGETIC

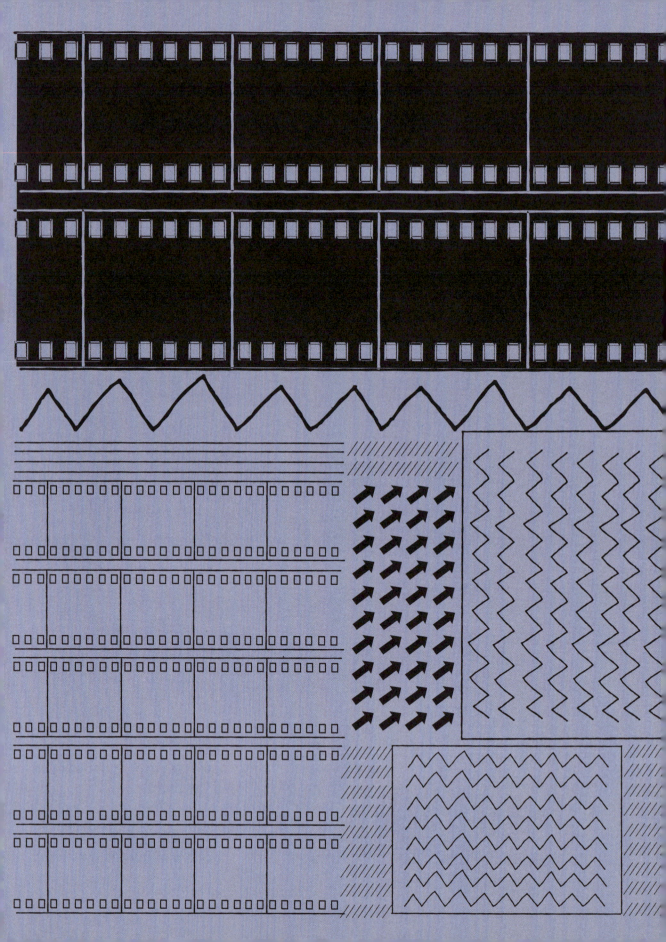

FILMANDTV

Film and TV are ways to tell stories using pictures, sounds, and actors. Movies are usually shown in theaters, while TV shows are watched at home on screens. They can make us laugh, cry, or even feel scared, and they let us visit new worlds or learn about real-life things. Film and TV are like magical windows that bring stories to life and keep us entertained!

skills

VISUAL THINKING

Filmmakers need to be able to imagine what a story will look like and communicate their vision to a whole team of people.

BIG PROJECTS

It can take many years for a movie to come to life. You must be patient and able to deal with changing situations.

STORYTELLING

Filmmakers have to find creative ways to tell their stories, through words, action moments, music, and mood.

IMAGINATION

You have to be able to dream big to create something that feels fresh and exciting to an audience!

You can make a movie just about anywhere —on the street in front of your house or in the halls of your school. When you're just getting started, you don't need any fancy equipment either—just a basic video camera. Someone's phone will do! Once you've got some footage captured, you're up and running! The first movie ever made was a short clip that showed a train arriving at a station. People were amazed by this magical moving picture! Now there are bustling film industries all around the world, and some of the most famous faces are the people we see on TV. But all kinds of people work behind the scenes in film to bring these big projects to life, from the people who write the scripts, to the people who coordinate big fight scenes. Here are a few of the jobs that make movies possible!

GARTH JENNINGS

DIRECTOR AND SCREENWRITER

Garth Jennings is a director and screenwriter. He has made music videos for artists including Blur, Radiohead, and Fatboy Slim. He directed *The Hitchhiker's Guide to the Galaxy*, and he wrote and directed the movies *Son of Rambo*, *Sing*, and *Sing 2*. He's also written three books about monsters and one about cowboys.

CAR WASH

In the hugely popular movies *Sing* and *Sing 2*, Garth was able to bring together his joint love of music and movies. As both scriptwriter and director, he worked alongside huge Hollywood stars including Matthew McConaughey and Scarlett Johannson, as well as the renowned musicians Halsey and Pharell Williams.

In the movie *Sing*, Garth voiced Miss Crawly, an elderly iguana who shares certain traits with Garth. They both like trainers. They're both forgetful and clumsy. But Garth is a little less green.

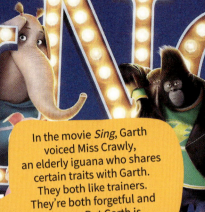

Pick-Up Shots

Quick shots to fill in the details of a scene. For example, close-ups of props or set-pieces.

Hi, I'm Garth. I make movies. I started making action movies when I was eleven with a secondhand camera that my dad bought. When I was a kid, I wanted to be a rock star, a film director, a puppeteer, a stuntman, a writer, an animator . . . Now I get to do almost all of that. Except being a stuntman. Call me if you need a stuntman.

WHAT'S THE BEST PART OF YOUR JOB?

A big part of the joy of filmmaking is working side by side with people who have exceptional talent. Editors, sound mixers, special effects, prop makers, stuntmen, caterers… everyone. There are hundreds of people in this industry who are incredibly talented in their specific field.

WHAT DOES A DIRECTOR DO?

A movie director decides what the movie will look like, how it will be shot, and how the actors will perform. I basically use cameras, actors, and special effects to bring stories to life and make you feel like you're right there with all the characters.

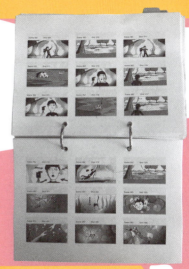

Crew Call

The time of day that shooting is scheduled to commence. Sometimes, it can be really early!

HOW DID YOU GET INTO ART SCHOOL?

My high-school exam scores were so blah and dreadful that I didn't have the grades required for art school. But I was desperate to go to art school, so I spent the summer drawing the best pictures I could. After several attempts at meeting the head of the art school, she finally agreed to see me on the strength of those drawings (and possibly just to get rid of me). She gave me a place on the art foundation course. This turned out to be the greatest year of my life.

Wrap

When a project or shoot is done. Time to celebrate!

JONNY MOORE

FILM SCULPTOR

Jonny Moore is a film sculptor, whose work has appeared in *Star Wars*, *Harry Potter*, and James Bond movies. Film sculptors work closely with filmmakers to create sculptures of people, animals, objects, or even landscapes that create the world of the film. They might work with clay, wood, metal, or plastic to get the right effect.

For the film *Death on the Nile*, Jonny led a team of twenty-five sculptors to recreate a life-size Egyptian temple. It was MASSIVE! It allowed the team to film in the UK to avoid concerns about logistics and heat.

DRAW ALL THE TIME, DRAW WHAT IS AROUND YOU, DRAW YOUR FAMILY AND FRIENDS, OR IF YOU LIVE NEAR A GOOD MUSEUM, GO AND SKETCH AN INTERESTING SCULPTURE.

Hi, I'm Jonny. When I was a kid, I thought I'd be a painter. I was constantly drawing and making things, so I've always been into it. At school, it was clearly my best subject and the only one I really enjoyed doing. One day, my tutor told me that sculpture was the hardest discipline in art. And I thought, "Alright! Bring it on!"

WHAT'S THE HARDEST THING ABOUT YOUR JOB?

Having to get up at the crack of dawn is not so great. The film industry starts early in the morning, so my alarm goes off at 5 a.m. every day. It also often involves a lot of smelly, dusty materials, so you have to be aware of the potential dangers.

Freestanding
refers to a sculpture not attached or supported by any other structure.

WHAT DEGREES DO YOU HAVE?

I left school at eighteen after my high-school exams and did a foundation course for a year, which was great because you try a bit of everything arts related and find out what you like best. I then moved to London to go to art college for five years! It was so exciting.

WHO ELSE DO YOU ADMIRE IN YOUR INDUSTRY?

Scenic painters are pretty amazing. Their job is to paint backdrops for around the edge of the stage, so it feels like the set continues off into the distance. Sometimes these paintings can be 30 feet tall and 100 feet long, and look even more realistic than a photo—but then when you get up close, they are rough, sketchy, and full of big, messy brush marks. It's like a really cool magic trick.

Relief
A type of sculpture where the shape itself is raised but still attached to a surface.

ERICA MCEWAN

CREATIVE DIRECTOR

Erica McEwan is a Creative Director at Painting Practice, a studio that creates designs for films and TV shows like *His Dark Materials*, *Wednesday*, and the new *Beauty and the Beast*. In the art department, Erica has used prop design and motion graphics to create authentic worlds, from giant wall designs to tiny soap dispensers.

Our work on *His Dark Materials* won a BAFTA award for Best Special, Visual, and Graphic Effects. We supported the Production Designer with very early concept drawings of towering city islands and armored bears, creating a design "blueprint" for the final visual effects.

© Bad Wolf.

WHAT ADVICE DO YOU HAVE FOR SOMEONE LOOKING TO WORK IN MOVIES?

You just have to start at the bottom. You have to make the tea, you have to say, "What can I do? Can I set up that table? Can I go pick up that thing?" You just have to be a Yes person, a Can-Do person. That is the best way to learn from others.

Hi, I'm Erica, and I make art for movies. When I was a growing up, I drew nonstop. My parents worked on events, and at the weekends I would have to go with them to their work. There were always loads of colored pens lying around, and I realized that someone was getting paid to use them. I thought, when I grow up, I could be a professional color-inner. In a way, I'm kind of doing that.

WHAT DEGREES DO YOU HAVE?

I did a degree in Visual Communication at the **University of Technology Sydney**, Australia. It was perfect because it gave me a springboard into typography, illustration, production design in film, motion graphics, and titles. There was a little bit of everything. In the third and fourth year, I focused a lot more on the film side.

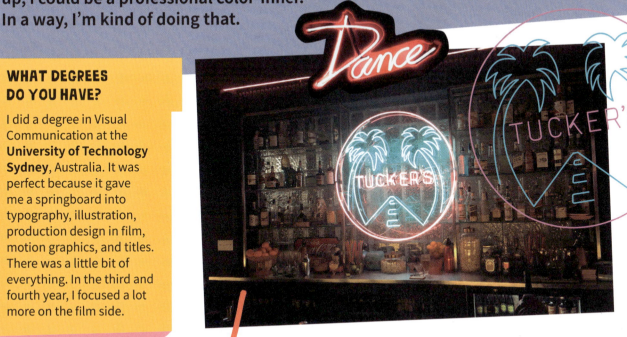

EVERY DOOR YOU OPEN FOR YOURSELF, THERE WILL BE MORE DOORS THAT WILL OPEN IN FRONT OF YOU AS WELL. SO BE BRAVE. YOU'VE GOT NOTHING TO LOSE REALLY, DO YOU?

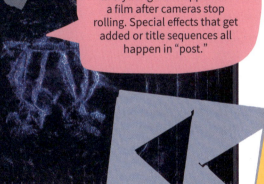

Postproduction

Everything that happens in a film after cameras stop rolling. Special effects that get added or title sequences all happen in "post."

WHAT WAS YOUR FIRST JOB?

I started volunteering on short films for free during college. I asked all my lecturers, "What are you working on? Can I come help you on the weekend?" I was very hungry to dive in really early. I started to see I had a knack for the art department and coming up with ideas. I would read scripts and be able to visualize how certain parts of the movie might look.

PIPS TAYLOR

BROADCASTER

Pips Taylor is a broadcaster who has fronted BBC documentaries, hosted huge programs like *The X Factor*, and interviewed famous musicians like Lizzo, Nile Rogers, Meghan Trainor, and Iggy Pop. Pips is also an in-demand DJ.

Pips hosted TEDxTeen, the teenage version of TED Talks, in London and New York. She interviewed teenagers from across the world who are changing the lives of their communities. The interviews took place in a big studio in front of a live audience. TEDxTeen was also filmed and released on a global live stream.

Runner

The typical starter job in television. It involves running errands and pitching in with whatever the crew need. You have to be alert and attentive!

CREATE YOUR OWN CONTENT, INTERVIEW YOUR FAMILY. GET COMFY IN FRONT OF THE CAMERA, AND TALK TO IT LIKE IT'S YOUR BEST FRIEND!

Hi, I'm Pips! I grew up in Bolton, UK, but after college, I moved to London to work in TV production. I started off as a runner, making teas and running around after the crew. I then became an Assistant Producer, booking talent for shows. While I did these jobs, I was also establishing my career as a presenter and interviewer—for example, by hosting the BRITs Red Carpet for a streaming brand and interviewing bands at music festivals.

WHAT'S YOUR ADVICE FOR GETTING INTO TV?

If you have a certain passion or are an expert in any area, such as music, art, or science, then that can help focus you on the direction of your career, including what type of programs you wish to make and present. It can feel like a constant hustle in terms of finding jobs, but there are agents who can help you.

Commissioners

People who decide what programs get made and when to release them. They listen to pitches from production teams and decide whether they want to show the program.

WHAT SKILLS DO YOU HAVE TO HAVE?

For me, a good TV presenter is someone who listens, is curious about people and the world, and who is passionate about helping others tell their stories. I also think being creative really helps, especially with researching your subject matter, writing scripts and interview questions. You can also write and develop ideas for programs and pitch them to TV channels and commissioners, too!

WHAT'S THE BEST THING ABOUT BEING A TV PRESENTER?

You get to work with lots of creative people. I love interviewing creatives, musicians, artists, and business owners—people from all walks of life. For me, a lot of work is project-based, so whether I'm hosting the Euros in front of thousands of attendees or presenting a series of shows on TV, I'll be meeting so many different people who all have their own story. They're usually very creative too, and that's where magic collaborations can happen!

THOMASINA SMITH

PAINTER AND DESIGNER

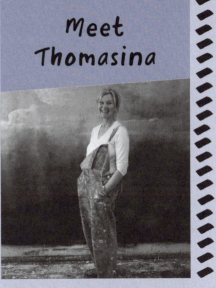

Thomasina's work is used in film, television, advertising, interior design, and theater. She has done commissions for films like *Notting Hill* and the Harry Potter series, as well as for The National Trust (historic houses), fashion house Emmanuel Ungaro, and interior designer Russell Sage.

For the film *Notting Hill*, Thomasina recreated a famous work called *La Mariée* by Marc Chagall. In order to get permission to use the painting in the movie, they had to agree to destroy Thomasina's copy, so that no one could try to sell it as a forgery!

The wizarding world of Hogwarts is bursting with magical moving portraits, and for the films, many of them were painted by Thomasina! She was one of several painters hired to create the paintings.

The National Portrait Gallery in London, UK, was one of the galleries that gave permission for the films to use certain paintings as inspiration. They came from a range of time periods and artists—one was an Elizabethan woman, another was by Velásquez, and one by Delacroix.

Hi, I'm Thomasina. When I was a kid, I used to play lots of imaginative games with my sister, like dress-up and turning our bedroom into a library. We painted and drew all day. I used to collect napkins, tickets, and postcards—anything with interesting lettering. I also loved the theater and would sometimes visit the paint frames behind the stage where backdrops and paintings were made for the set. I now get to work on paintings for amazing films and with brilliant musicians like Florence and the Machine.

HOW DID YOU START OUT IN THIS JOB?

I worked on anything I could in the early days—jobs like mine aren't always advertised! So it was a matter of getting to know people. I worked hard to build a professional reputation, and I tried to be reliable and helpful as well as creative. I would even volunteer on low-budget art films, and that ended up paying off—the people in charge would go on to work on bigger productions and would remember me.

Replica

Something made to closely resemble something else. For example, a replica of a painting by Renoir would look as close as possible to the original.

WHAT MAKES FOR A GOOD SCENIC DESIGNER?

Stay curious and interested in the world! Immerse yourself in culture and history, and read, read, read. See as much as you can, and let it feed your creativity. You also need to be organized and disciplined. Films often work on tight timelines.

WHAT IS ONE OF YOUR FAVORITE PROJECTS?

I was asked to make the paintings for a movie about Francis Bacon, an Irish-British painter whose style was very dark. While working on it, I realized it combined my love of making things, my love of performing arts, and my passion for Art History. It was a perfect project for me.

Backdrop

A large-scale photo or painting that creates a location for a scene using cloth or canvas. Often they are lit up to look like the outdoors.

ALWAYS CARRY A SMALL PENCIL CASE CONTAINING:

1 sharpener

2 pencils
(one fine and one thick)

3 ink pen

4 eraser

THE LOVEGOOD HOUSE

For *Harry Potter and the Deathly Hallows: Part One*, Thomasina was commissioned to paint the home of Luna Lovegood, a quirky, dreamy young witch.

The art department imagined that the house would be covered in drawings of magical animals, and they put together references of primitive art and lists of animals from *Fantastic Beasts and Where to Find Them*.

Thomasina wanted to give the feeling that Luna had made the drawings as a girl, so she spoke with Evanna Lynch, the actor who played Luna. Evanna drew some pictures of the set, to give Thomasina a feel for how Evanna expressed herself artistically.

Mural
A painting made directly onto a wall or set piece. Can be used for films as well as street art.

Thomasina then began making black-and-white concept sketches of the animals. She also created a model box for the interior of the house (using the actual material of the set) and made rough paintings of the creatures.

When it came time to paint onto the actual set, Thomasina had to use a cherry picker to paint the exterior of the house, because it was so big!

MIKE SKRGATIC

VISUAL EFFECTS ARTIST (VFX)

Mike Skrgatic is the cofounder of Time Based Arts, a trailblazing VFX (visual effects) company based in the heart of London. Their work has spanned everything from short commercials, to music videos and major motion pictures. Recently, he has helped the UK's Channel 4 develop their new station idents to reflect the diversity of life in the UK!

Meet Mike

Mike cocreated the new idents for Channel 4. He spent twelve months working on the project, coming up with the idea, developing it creatively, producing and shooting it, then doing the special effects. He led seventeen directors and hundreds of creative makers to bring it to life!

IF YOU DON'T QUITE FIT INTO THE CURRENT SCHOOL SYSTEM—YOU'LL MORE THAN LIKELY FIT IN TO THE CREATIVE INDUSTRIES.

Idents
The ways that TV and radio stations identify themselves, so that you know what channel you're playing.

Hey, I'm Mike. Some people think kids should all study math to high-school level, but I think all kids should be studying art. Everyone would benefit from doing a foundation course in art at some point in life. I actually studied Tapestry. I didn't do any traditional weaving, but chose the course because of the open-mindedness of the tutors and the fact that they let us express ourselves in any way we chose.

WHAT MAKES A GOOD VFX DESIGNER?

VFX is the ultimate team sport. It's all about collaboration and good communication. Having a technical mind helps, but for me creative flare is by far the most important aspect. Having the ability to access an image, such as a painting, and then adapt and embellish that painting to make it better is a big part of the job.

Color Grading

After a film has finished production, it will go through this process to adjust the colors of the film for different environments and devices.

VFX

Stands for visual effects. Filmmakers use computer images that would be dangerous or expensive or impossible to film live.

ANY TIPS FOR ASPIRING YOUNG VFX AARTISTS?

Learn to shoot stills, and film for yourself. Understanding other areas of the filmmaking process and how images are made will make you a better artist. Knowing camera techniques, lensing, and shoot terminology will help you to understand and collaborate with others, and plan your your VFX shots. Think outside the box; don't always rely on the tricks and tools available in the software.

WOULD YOU CHANGE ANYTHING ABOUT HOW YOU STARTED YOUR CAREER?

I probably would have taken time out to experience life a bit longer. I went straight from school to college and straight from college into my career. Real-life experience makes you a more rounded artist and will give you more to say. Travel and see the world: It will give you a wiser perspective and a better understanding of who you are and the values that matter.

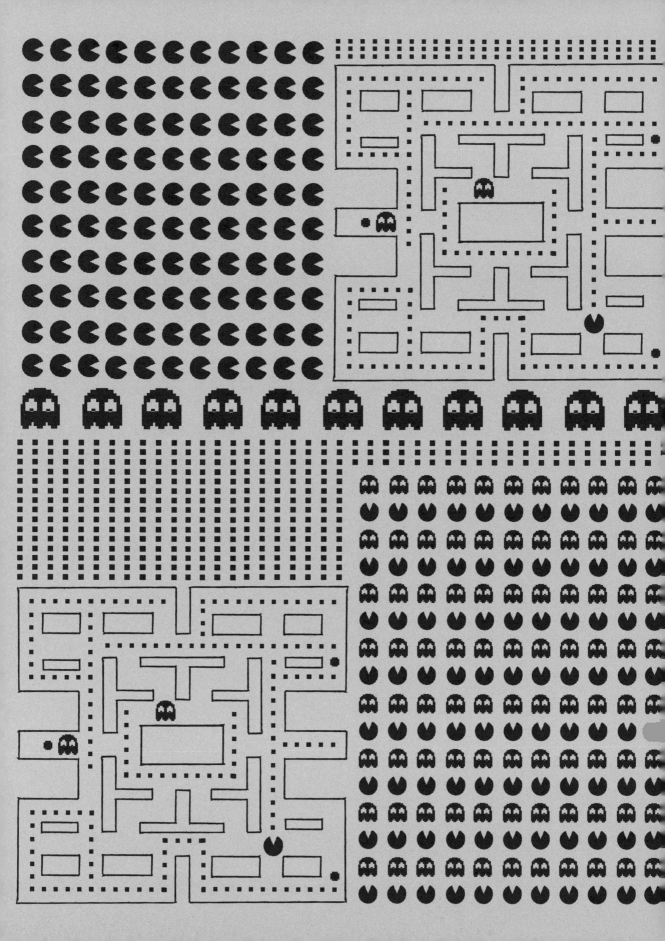

GAMES

Toys and games involve designers of all types to create an experience that feels fun and seamless! For toys, designers decide what materials are used, how a toy will work, and what it will sound like if it makes sounds. For video games, designers create the world, the characters, and the rules of the game.

skills

LOGIC

Game designers need to think a lot about rules. Often, it's the limitations in games that can make them so tricky and fun.

WORLD-BUILDING

Video game designers need to create worlds that completely immerse you, with great characters, locations, and rules.

CHARACTER DESIGN

In a game, you often get to create your own character. Game artists have to come up with building blocks that can be interchangeable!

PLAYFULNESS

It's vital that game and toy designers are able to find the fun! What makes you laugh or keeps you entertained?

Think about your favorite toy or game. What makes it fun? Is it something that you can play with your friends, or is it more of a solo game? Do you pretend to be a character when you're playing it, or are you just yourself? Does it go by quickly, or does it take a long time? How do the colors and sounds it makes create a mood?

Designers of toys and games have to answer all of these questions in order to create things that YOU will want to play with again and again.

DANNY GRAY

CHIEF CREATIVE OFFICER

Danny Gray is the Chief Creative Officer at ustwo games. He leads the creative vision of the studio and works on directing the production of award-winning games such as *Monument Valley* and *Assemble with Care*. When directing games, it is his job to envisage the whole game in his head and devise the steps to get there

I GOT TOLD A LOT WHEN I WAS YOUNGER NOT TO PURSUE MAKING GAMES. BUT I WAS STUBBORN ABOUT IT. IF IT'S SOMETHING YOU REALLY BELIEVE IS GOING TO MAKE YOU HAPPY, DON'T LET OTHER PEOPLE DICTATE THAT FOR YOU.

For the launch of *Monument Valley 2*, the ustwo team partnered with visual artist Alex Yanes to create an installation on Coney Island. This venture was part of a "**celebration of creativity,**" using the game as inspiration for all kinds of artists in other fields.

#MONUMENTVALLEY2

Hey, I'm Danny. Growing up outside Manchester, UK, I remember I was at my grandma's house with a few other cousins. One of my cousins was like, "I want to be a fireman," and one said, "I want to be a space man." And all the adults were laughing, and I said, "I want to make computer games." They continued laughing. So I went into my grandma's kitchen and wrote a note on her noticeboard that said: "I want to make computer games." She kept it her whole life.

WAS IT DIFFICULT TO GET INTO THE GAMES INDUSTRY?

Yeah. It was really, really difficult. Now, there are lots of smaller indie games studios, so there's more roles you can apply for. But luckily, one of my favorite games studios, Lionshead Studios, had a work experience opportunity doing Quality Assurance for one week. I had a girlfriend at the time who lived nearby. I stayed with her parents and made a two-and-a-half-hour journey there and back every day. But I did the week and was fortunate enough to get a job at the end of it.

Quality Assurance
This is about finding the problems in software and communicating what they are. In games, it might mean playing a game to test that everything works.

Indie
A small games studio that doesn't have the backing of a big games publisher. They can be more creative and experimental, and lots are thriving in the USA and the UK.

WHAT DID YOU STUDY?

I was a very average student. I got a B in IT and a B in Art in high school. At the time, I wanted to go to college, as none of my family had ever been. I ended up at a university in Leeds doing Computer Entertainment Technology. And for the first time, my grades were good. Because it was way more hands-on and vocational. I wasn't the most book-academic person, I was more of a doer.

WHAT DOES AN AVERAGE DAY LOOK LIKE FOR YOU?

I start with a stand-up with my project team. We talk about what we did yesterday, what we're going to do today. Hopefully, I'll have an hour of time afterward to work on story stuff: writing or research. Maybe I'll design some screens and figure out what the user flow might be like. I might also have to do some company stuff, like talking about hiring or partnerships. I might go play the latest version of another team's game and give them feedback.

I just hope I can do this

MONUMENT VALLEY
BY USTWO GAMES

HOW THEY MADE IT

1

PROTOTYPE

Over the course of one week, the team of twenty people in the studio built a prototype of the game.

They began bending the rules of space to allow the architecture to do unexpected things. They decided that players could interact with the architecture using their fingers, revealing paths they didn't know were there.

IDA

CROW

2

CHARACTERS

Next, the team created Ida: a small, geometric character that travels through the buildings. They wanted her to be a blank canvas—to become whatever the player wanted her to be.

They created crow characters, which were the opposite of Ida, with the pointed cone as a beak rather than a hat.

3

LEVELS

They created levels with different themes, so that the players would feel like they were making progress and opening doors to new challenges.

No enemies, they decided, and no scores or ticking clocks. No pressure. Just solving impossible problems in a beautiful world. Go on, check it out!

UX AND GAMES

In most video games, a player is dropped into
a totally new, immersive world and given
a challenge that they need to solve.
But when you're starting off a game, how do you know
what to do? UX (or User eXperience) designers work
to make games easy to navigate, creating key
features like menus, buttons, and maps.
When players can find tools and resources easily,
they feel more at home in the world of the game
and will want to stay in it and
keep playing!

Crypto Garden

May Villani

May Villani is the Product Design Director at Netspeak Games. She runs a team of UX and UI designers based around the world who make multiplayer social games. Their first one, *Sunshine Days*, is about building a village together. For this project, May had to think about tools that would help users collaborate and communicate with each other effectively. Every day, she asks herself these questions:

UX designers have to think every day about how to make their worlds a better place for users—to be accessible and friendly, with clear rules and ways to get around.

In her free time, May reads lots of books about psychology, human behavior, and communication.

"When I discovered that there was a job that could marry these interests with games," she said, "I knew it was my destiny."

Is this button useful to users?

What do these people need?

Is this feature well understood?

Could this feature hurt or neglect some users?

I ADVOCATE FOR PLAYERS.
IN EVERYTHING I DO, I TRY TO FOCUS ON THE USER PERSPECTIVE.
CONSTANT EMPATHY IS THE WAY TO GO.

GRAPHICDESIGN

Graphic designers communicate ideas to help people understand or feel something. They use text, images, colors and illustrations to create unique designs that inform and help you differentiate one brand from another. Graphics are everywhere, and as communication evolves through digital and social forms, it means that graphic design is a much-needed skill.

These designs will cover things you see and use every day, such as food packaging, logos and branding, and book designs. You will also encounter it digitally on websites and mobile interfaces on your devices, plus places you may not think of, such as fashion graphics or title sequences in film and on TV.

skills

COLORS

Graphic designers have a strong sense of how different colors (and shades!) make you feel, as well as which ones pair well together.

FONTS AND LETTERING

Can you tell the difference between silly letters and serious ones? Each has their own place. DIFFERENT FONTS make you feel *DIFFERENT THINGS*.

CARTOONS

Often, graphic designers will use cartoons to get a point across, maybe even creating a mascot for a brand that people will recognize and remember.

PROBLEM-SOLVING

Graphic designers have to work with constraints: small spaces, strict guidelines, project timelines. A good designer knows how to adapt!

GRAPHIC DESIGN IS EVERYWHERE

Everyone loves graphic design—and the demand has never been higher. Using colors and fonts to communicate is a skill that many designers use every single day—so keep your eye out for graphic experts hidden in other industries throughout this book!

INSPIRATION: TYPESCRIPTS!

Helvetica is one of the most popular typeface in the world. It was developed in 1957 by Swiss designers Max Miedinger and Eduard Hoffmann, who wanted a font that could be used on many different kinds of signs. Since then, it's been used on the NASA Space Shuttle orbiter, the Swiss soccer uniform, and road signs all over the world.

FILM AND TV

Just like the real world, film worlds are full of text that gives you information about where you are. **Erica McEwan** creates graphics that define the spirit of award-winning TV shows like *Black Mirror*.

FASHION

Asya Smailbegovic uses graphics to create hip prints for clothing. She'll often play with contrasts, using cute, old-fashioned designs to say something a little bit rude!

RETAIL SPACES

At Accept & Proceed, **Matt Jones** used moving typography to make retail spaces dynamic and modern. At Nike's store in Paris, they used graphic visualizations to bring Nike's Training Club data to life.

GRAPHIC DESIGN in...

DIGITAL

Dines uses his graphics training to create fresh digital designs that help brands express where they fit into new cultural movements. His designs are all about connecting a product, company, or musician with the world that young people are experiencing today.

BRANDING

Brand designer **Dave Rax** designs graphic treatments and fonts that you see on products like Fanta all over the world. Often, he is working with brands that have been around for awhile, in order to make their look more modern and accessible.

ILLUSTRATION

Printmaker **Rose Stallard** uses graphics all the time in her work to create funky, rock 'n' roll messages for her prints. Her typography is inspired by 1970s fanzines (or fan magazines), which used jagged, punky combinations of text and images to capture the spirit of an exciting movement.

RUDE

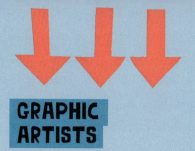

Meet Abi & Rupert

Rude is a London-based graphic and illustration studio founded by Rupert and Abi Meats. Over three decades their distinctive colorful style has covered all areas of graphic design: 2D and 3D, moving and static, analog and digital. From packaging to animations, murals, book and record sleeve design, the duo have covered it all. In fact, they designed this very book you're reading.

Hi, I'm Rupert. For as long as I remember, I've wanted to make things, draw, and create. I can't imagine doing anything else. On my Art Foundation course, I had a tutor who was a printmaker. I was obsessed with the aesthetic of screen printing, and the way you can imagine an image and then put it onto paper.

BE THE MOST EXCELLENT THAT YOU CAN BE. BEING MEDIOCRE ISN'T GOOD ENOUGH. Rupert

Hi, I'm Abi. When I was little, my aunty was an actress, and I went to see her in a play in London. On the Tube were the posters for all the West End theater shows. One of them, for the English National Opera (or the ENO), had a swoosh of paint that looked like a caped figure. I had a full body reaction to it. I loved their little logo that looked like someone singing but was made out of only three letters (ENO). It was the cleverest thing I'd ever seen.

YOU HAVE TO BE RESILIENT, YOU HAVE TO HUSTLE, AND YOU HAVE TO BE TRUE TO YOURSELF. Abi

BRAND & ADVERTISING

ARCHITECTURE

VISUAL ARTS

CRAFTS

GRAPHICS

FASHION

FILM & TV

MUSIC

COSTUME

PHOTOGRPAHY

PUBLISHING

DIGITAL

TOYS /GAMES

PRODUCT DESIGN

MUSEUMS & GALLERIES

PERFORMING ARTS

UNLEASH YOUR CREATIVE SUPERPOWERS

That's exactly how this book came to life! We gave it a name, made sure it was fun and easy to read, and designed it to inspire and inform YOU about creative jobs. We wanted it to be bold, colorful, and exciting. Every part of the design was carefully chosen to make the book easy to explore. Here are some key design elements we used:

BOOK COVER

This is often the hardest part of the project to get right since it has to have shelf appeal and stand out from all other books. A quick glance at the cover should immediately tell the reader what the book is about.

COLOR PALETTE

Colors help you know where you are in the book! We've assigned main colors to different sections, with extra colors to support them.

TYPOGRAPHY

This is all about fonts! We even hand-drew a playful one that looks like a child made it. We mixed it with other easy-to-read fonts, using bold ones for headlines.

ICONS

These are little pictures that show information or ideas.

LOCKUPS

Think of these as handy labels or headers that appear throughout the book to guide you through.

BORDERS & FRAMES

These are illustrations that decorate the edges of pages and make them stand out!

EVERYTHING IN THIS BOOK WAS DESIGNED ESPECIALLY FOR YOU!

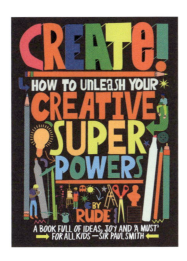

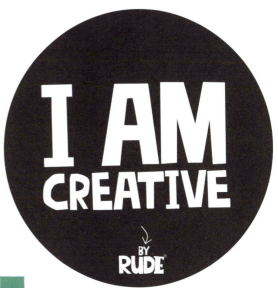

I AM CREATIVE

BY RUDE

CREATE!

UNLEASH YOUR CREATIVE SUPERPOWERS

AN INTRODUCTION TO CREATIVE CAREERS

BRAND AND ADVERTISING

I AM CREATIVE

1 2 3 4 5 6 7 8 9 10

a B C D E F G H

SHION

TOYS & GAMES

COSTUME

GRAPHICS

FILM & TV

VISUAL ARTS

DIGITAL

PUBLISHING

MUSEUMS & GALLERIES

PRODUCT DESIGN

RAFTS

PHOTOGRAPHY

PERFORMING ARTS

ARCHITECTURE

MUSIC

BRAND & ADVERTISING

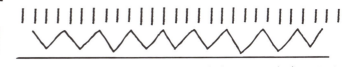

MUSEUMS AND GALLERIES

Art is designed to be seen—and the best way for artists to become well known is for their work to be seen by as many people as possible. Enter museums and galleries: These special spaces work with artists to showcase their work to people who will be affected by it—and maybe even want to buy it!

SKILLS

WRITING

Museum curators often have to get many advanced degrees and be able to communicate their ideas clearly in academic writing.

HISTORY

A good museum worker can understand how the art or artifacts they are showing fit into a bigger historical picture.

TEACHING

You have to be able to explain to a museum audience why a particular artist or movement was important!

SPATIAL SKILLS

A curator must understand how artworks will work within their particular space. How will the light or the size of the room affect the art?

Museums come in many varieties—some are privately owned, others are free to the public. Some have unique, specific collections, while others have items and artworks that span hundreds—if not millions—of years! Museum Mile in London, UK, might have thirteen world-class destinations, but cities all across the world have their own incredible museums, such as the Brooklyn Museum in New York, the Art Gallery of Ontario in Canada, and the New Orleans Museum of Art in Louisiana. Find out where your closest museums are, and go explore their latest exhibitions. Think about the items that were chosen to be shown and why they are arranged in the way that they are.

OCKI MAGILL

GALLERY OWNER

Ocki runs Blue Shop Cottage in London, UK. Blue Shop is warm and approachable. They believe in the power of community—providing social engagement and inspiration for artists and collectors. Their openings are always filled to the rafters with buzzing, laughing people, and their artist talks are free for anyone to attend.

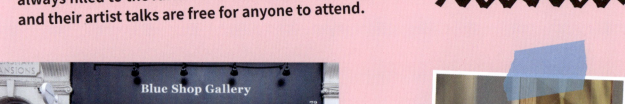

In November 2023, Ocki opened a second gallery with a first show by **Jess Allen**. Jess's work is all about honoring everyday, overlooked things: books, empty seats, the shadows of people together. She sold out every piece.

Hi, I'm Ocki. I've always loved artists and paintings and the history of art. In 2016, I bought an old shop and lived there with my dog Mole. We tried many things: mini concerts, a flower shop, a bike shop, a cocktail bar. One day I thought, "Maybe we could start selling art!" In 2018, we made a lovely film and poster and held our very first exhibition. We sold artwork to lots of happy collectors, and that was the beginning of Blue Shop Cottage.

WHAT DEGREES DO YOU HAVE?

I studied Fashion Design: Womenswear at **Central Saint Martins** in the UK, followed by Graphic Design and Art Direction in Sydney, Australia. I also worked for Christopher Raeburn and Kristjana S. Williams doing pattern cutting and design for them.

WHAT QUALITIES DO YOU HAVE TO HAVE AS A GALLERIST?

I love combining my design and creative direction skills with being a people person. I was brought up to bring people together—my parents both do that for their families—they are the central roof under which everyone meets and embraces. This is really what I do with Blue Shop. I love people, and I really do believe in their power to inspire others.

Collector
Someone who invests in artwork. A good gallerist will get to know collectors and their individual tastes.

Framing
The art of customizing a structure to frame an artist's work and show it in its best light.

HOW DO YOU WORK WITH ARTISTS?

You have to be genuinely inspired by the art you are showing. It's important to understand the artist and what they want to get out of a show, and by hanging out with them and their work, you can help them tell the story of the show. Understanding the collector is also really important: knowing what they're looking for, what services they want, and how you can support them to find works for their collection.

ON OUR OPENING NIGHT, I REMEMBER STANDING BACK FOR A MOMENT AWAY FROM THE CROWDS, SEEING EVERYONE THERE, SELLING BEAUTIFUL ARTWORK AND MAKING AN EMERGING ARTIST VERY HAPPY. I KNEW I HAD STARTED A BUSINESS DOING ALL OF THE THINGS I LOVE MOST.

ART HISTORY AND CURATION

For many roles in museums today, especially in art curation, an advanced degree in Art History has become a must. Art historians begin by looking at the surface appearance of an artwork, and then they explore all of the complex influences behind its production: the background of the artist, social ideas and artistic movements at the time, materials that were popular or available for use. Today, when art historians curate exhibitions, many think about how to make historical artworks exciting for audiences today, and they tell stories about how different pieces of art influence and react to each other.

Sayantan Mukhopadhyay

Sayantan Mukhopadhyay is the Assistant Curator of Modern and Contemporary Art at the Portland Museum of Art in Maine, USA. He has worked all over the world in different jobs relating to art and culture, including in Shanghai, Delhi, and New York. His work has focused on modern art from South Asia, queer history, and photography—and where these things overlap.

Sayantan began his career working in art galleries, but he wanted to deal more with the history and theory of art. He studied for a PhD in Art History, focusing on radical artwork about the nation of India in the 1980s and 1990s. At the **Portland Museum of Art**, he helps create conversations around art that tell stories outside the dominant culture. This requires a lot of deep thinking and research!

"Exhibitions you see at places like the Tate or the Metropolitan Museum have taken years and years to develop," he says. "Tenacity is essential!"

DON'T STUDY AN ARTIST, TIME PERIOD, CULTURE, OR MOVEMENT BECAUSE YOU THINK IT WILL GET YOU A JOB, BUT RATHER BECAUSE YOU ARE DEEPLY INTERESTED IN IT.
THAT PASSION WILL ALWAYS SHINE THROUGH.

THE ART OF COLLECTING

In the sixteenth century, German people began to collect notable items in wardrobes that they called *Wunderkammer*, meaning "cabinets of curiosities." Collectors had various motivations: to show status, loyalty, or attraction, or merely to satisfy a habit. Naturally, a large collection with rare items begins to gain new value—being able to compare similar objects allows us to learn more about the category of the collection. Some of the most high-value collectors today purchase art, stamps, or coins. But an amateur collector can begin with things that are entirely free: interesting seashells, sugar packets, autographs. Eventually, your collection might be interesting enough to have in a museum!

Chelsea-Louise Berlin

When Chelsea-Louise was going out to club nights and parties from 1986 onward, she began collecting flyers. She'd be offered them as she entered a club or left one, in record stores, or in art exhibits. They were fascinating items of pop culture, the entry to many a night of fun. She kept the items as historic mementoes and began to build her own visual library, alongside abstract drawings that she made of people dancing in the clubs.

Over time, the flyers became a valuable resource for social history, graphic art, and popular culture. Chelsea-Louise's collection of artifacts grew to more than 10,000 pieces of pop memorabilia and socially historic graphic art—and she wanted to share it.

INTERPRET WHAT YOU SEE, HEAR & FEEL, AND TURN IT INTO SOMETHING TANGIBLE FOR OTHERS TO ENJOY & BE MOVED BY.

Chelsea-Louise Berlin

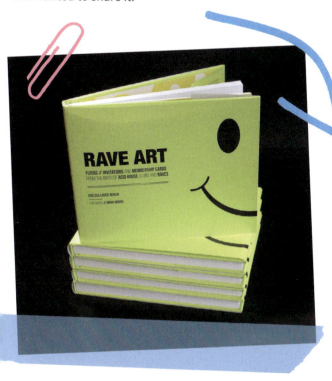

At first, she thought about a book and was commissioned to write *Rave Art* for Welbeck Publishing Group. Then, she was commissioned to create an installation at the **Saatchi Gallery** in London that showcased more than 1,500 of her flyers and artifacts. The exhibit emphasized how electronic music brought people together from all walks of life: It was an incredible way for her physical collection to be experienced anew.

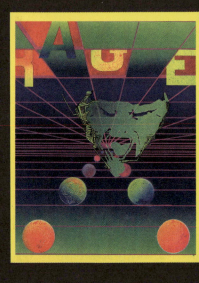

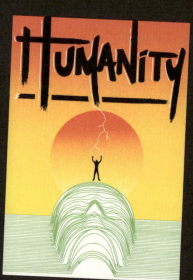

Technicolor synthesiser.
Zak Norman. ©

- MUSIC -

MUSIC

Music is the art of making sounds that we love to listen to, like songs, beats, and melodies. Musicians use songs to express feelings, tell a story, or create a mood. Have you ever tried to make up a song to show how you're feeling? Or to make someone laugh? Learning to play an instrument at school is often the best way to get going!

SKILLS

PLAYING AN INSTRUMENT

You may want to try a few different instruments to find the one that best fits how you want to express yourself!

TEAMWORK

Even solo musicians have to be able to work with a whole team of people in order to play on stages and get their music recorded!

SONGWRITING

If you can make up a tune and write lyrics that fit with the feeling of it, you may find you have a talent for songwriting.

PERSISTENCE

Musicians have to stay motivated and keep their self-belief, even when they have a hard time finding opportunities to play.

Listen to your favorite song. How do you think it was made? One singer or two? Can you hear live instruments, or does it have a more electronic beat? Today, musicians come in many flavors—they might sing or play an instrument, or they might create beats from software. Sometimes they write their own songs, and sometimes they work with other people. The music industry is also full of lots of talented people behind the scenes: Sound recordists, producers who put together different talented artists, and DJs who take different tracks and remix them to create something totally new.

BICEP

DJ DUO

Belfast-born Andy Ferguson and Matt McBriar from Ireland form Bicep, a DJ duo who produce electronic music and play live sets. Together, they have headlined major British festivals and toured around the world. Their music is all about creating an atmosphere for dancing, and they often work with visual artists to create mind-blowing effects for their shows.

Festival

An organized series of concerts and entertainment, usually held every year in the same place. In the US, they range from giant festivals like **Coachella in California** to smaller festivals such as **Newport Folk Festival**.

In 2022, Bicep was the closing act of the West Holts stage at **Glastonbury**. "It's still a blur, to be honest," they said. The BBC said that this performance "cemented their names as one of the biggest names in UK dance."

WHAT IS IT LIKE WORKING WITH A FRIEND?

Opposites work well, but it's important to respect each other's decisions or opinions. Bringing together multiple ideas and feelings always yields the most interesting results.

DJ

Short for Disc Jockey, coined by an American radio commentator in the 1930s. DJs create a seamless mix of music for dancing.

Hey, we're Matt and Andy. Music was a huge part of both our upbringing in Ireland. We're both from families where music was just around us all day long. In our teens, we messed about with some production programs, but we only started to take it more seriously once we got into our early 20s. Initially, it grew from a desire to reedit and remix for DJing. Slowly, we wanted more input and developed a hunger to be artists ourselves.

WHAT DEGREES DID YOU STUDY?

Matt: I studied Graphic Design for my degree. It was quite a conceptual course, teaching us to think creatively. I draw on what I learned there almost daily.

Andy: I got a Chemical Engineering degree from the **University of Manchester** in the UK. To be honest, the degree was not something I loved. But it really taught me about perseverance in trying to work at something, and it ultimately gave me problem-solving skills—particularly in solving large complex problems as an individual or a group.

IF YOU DIDN'T DO YOUR JOB, WHAT WOULD YOU DO?

Matt: I'd maybe work in food, but it's possibly even worse hours than music, ha ha!

Andy: I always wanted to be a product designer from when I was a young kid. I still feel it's an area in which I could work. It would probably be on the more aesthetic rather than the functional side.

RAE MORRIS

SINGER-SONGWRITER

Rae Morris is a singer-songwriter from Blackpool, UK. Her first album, *Unguarded*, reached the UK Top 10 in the official albums chart. Since then, she has released three other studio albums and performed at huge UK festivals like Bestival, Glastonbury, Reading, and All Points East.

I DON'T BELIEVE YOU HAVE TO BE THE BEST AT ANYTHING. I THINK IT'S THE PEOPLE THAT HAVE SELF-BELIEF AND PASSION FOR THEIR CRAFT THAT GET THEMSELVES TO WHERE THEY WANT TO BE.

Rae released *Unguarded* when she was twenty-three years old. Rae's impressive vocals tie the whole album together, though the songs are a real mix of dance-floor pop and big emotional piano tracks. Go take a listen!

Royalties

The money that somebody earns from a song when they own the copyright. This could be when somebody streams a recording of the song or lets someone else make a record of it.

Hi, I'm Rae. I started playing piano when I was really young, then when I was around seventeen years old, I started writing songs. I would go to open mic nights where anyone could get up and perform. When people seemed to enjoy the music I was making, I started to imagine that songwriting and performing might be something I could do more of. Not long after that, I started to be contacted by record labels.

WHAT DEGREES DO YOU HAVE?

I did music in high school but I didn't go to college. I got a place at the brilliant **Leeds College of Music**, but around that time, I signed my first record deal with **Atlantic Records** instead. My journey then became more about practical learning on the go and spending lots of time honing the craft, before putting out a debut album four years later.

Record Label
A company that signs up musicians to record and promote their music in exchange for a percentage of the money that the artist makes from their songs.

HOW WOULD YOU DESCRIBE YOUR STYLE AS A MUSICIAN?

My music and performance style is inspired by the great trailblazing artists of the past (female artists like Kate Bush, Carole King, and Björk), combined with modern technology and ways of recording. I love the classic sound of a simple piano and vocal, but then like to take the listener out of that moment by doing something unexpected with an exciting sound they've never heard before!

WAS IT HARD TO BECOME A PROFESSIONAL MUSICIAN?

Getting into any creative industry requires a combination of hard work and luck. In the beginning, I played hundreds of small gigs to get my name out there and find opportunities. I put everything else on hold in my life to do that —including not hanging out with my friends as much as the average seventeen-year-old would. If I were to do it all again, I'd try to make time for myself in those early years.

NIGEL ADAMS

RECORD LABEL OWNER

Nigel co-owns and runs two record labels: Full Time Hobby and Hassle Records. He is also a music publisher and manages several artists, including Dana Gavanski and Bananagun. His job involves finding and signing new acts, overseeing recording and writing projects, managing the money and legal issues, organizing the musicians' visual art and live events, and coordinating promotion, marketing, and distribution of albums. Phew!

Full Time Hobby represents Pale Blue Eyes, a band from Devon, UK, who in eighteen months went from playing tiny pub venues to headlining **Village Underground**, a giant warehouse in the center of London. Rock on!

A&R
A&R means Artists and Repertoire, the part of a music label that is responsible for finding and developing new acts.

Hey, I'm Nigel. As a teenager, I was obsessed with music and spent much of my early years seeing bands, making music, buying records, talking about bands, and playing records with friends. I soon realized I was obsessed beyond just being a fan and wanted to do whatever it took to get more involved in the process of getting new music out into the world. I loved finding new, unheard-of bands and getting other people excited about them, too.

Indie

Independent record labels are smaller, scrappier operations than major record labels, and they often sign cutting-edge acts.

HOW DID YOU GET STARTED?

In my early twenties, I began promoting bands and doing some music journalism. I don't think I originally approached it as looking for a job, I couldn't help myself from being involved in music in whatever form—buying, listening, gigging, or writing. Through that, I landed my first job as an assistant at a US indie label.

WHAT DO YOU LOOK FOR IN A MUSICIAN?

The best artists are those that really immerse themselves in their craft and have an opinion, not just on the music they are producing, but the visual side, too, and how that all fits into culture in general. They need to be great songwriters but also compelling when performing live. They should have the ability to connect with universal truths via their music.

ANY ADVICE FOR ASPIRING RECORD LABEL EXECS?

Get involved in music any way you can to start with. Learn about the different areas in the music industry—put on gigs, write reviews, listen to lots of music, go to gigs. Share your passion with others, and connect with people who feel the same way about music. Help people out, and be kind.

A LOT OF IT IS ABOUT TIMING AND STRATEGY—HELPING THE ARTISTS TO REALLY MAKE THE MOST OF THEIR TALENTS AND PROVIDING THEM WITH A SUPPORT NETWORK.

POLITICS AND MUSIC

Music (and art in general!) has long been a vehicle for expressing messages of HOPE, FREEDOM, and SOCIAL JUSTICE. Many artists and musicians use their talents to advocate for a world in which everyone gets equal rights and opportunities, and **to give voice to people who often can't speak for themselves.**

Music was a huge part of the Civil Rights Movement with artists like Sam Cooke, Mahalia Jackson, and Bob Dylan singing about change to boost morale at protests. Fighting for change is never easy, but music can often be a way to unite people and keep their spirits up, even in the darkest moments.

Naomi Larsson Piñeda

Naomi is a British-Chilean musician and an award-winning journalist. As an artist, she performs under Naomi in Blue and sometimes with the band La Chinaca. Her first EP, *An Experiment*, was released in 2021. She has worked as a writer and editor for *gal-dem* magazine and *The Guardian*, and her reporting on Chile was shortlisted for an Amnesty Media Award.

In Chile, Naomi has been able to combine her passion for social justice with her musical gifts. After a recent gig in Santiago, she felt:

"It was really special to see how my music has managed to travel across the world and still touch people, even in a different language."

Through both her writing and her music, Naomi promotes fairness for all people. Even within the music industry, she tries to build communities that support female musicians and advocates for safer, more equal spaces.

MUSIC HAS ALWAYS INFORMED MY JOURNALISM, AND VICE VERSA. I USE SONGWRITING AS STORYTELLING, PARTICULARLY INFLUENCED BY THE PEOPLE I'VE MET AND THE STORIES I'VE TOLD THROUGH JOURNALISM.

PERFORMING ARTS

Do you love being in the spotlight? Know how to make people laugh? Performers are people who use their bodies and voices as instruments to tell stories, express themselves, and entertain others. They might be dancers or actors or singers—or maybe even all three!

SKILLS

CHARISMA

Being able to charm your audience is important—they must be on your side! A sense of humor helps, as does knowing when to drop the perfect punchline.

MOVEMENT

Dancers have total mastery of their bodies, but all great performers have a sense of how to achieve an effect with movement.

SELF-EXPRESSION

A good performer always speaks from the heart, even when they are playing a character. That way, they will connect with the audience.

MEMORY

Many performers have to memorize scripts or sheet music as a part of their job. This will take hours and hours of practice!

The performing arts is a great way to connect with other people who all want to create something together. Across the world, the performing arts have been thriving for centuries and are a major part of culture, even in small towns. Often, even in productions designed for adults, there are roles for kids. Is there a local theater near you? Next time you go, wait at the stage door afterward and you might get to talk to some of the performers (or at the very least, get their autograph).

ELEANOR WYLD

ACTOR AND WRITER

Eleanor Wyld is an actor and a writer. Her acting roles have included characters in plays, movies, and TV shows. Actors use their voices, bodies, and faces to make people believe that they are someone else. Eleanor has acted in TV shows like *Black Mirror* and *Lovesick*.

JUST DO IT! SEIZE EVERY OPPORTUNITY WHATEVER YOU CAN, WHENEVER YOU CAN. LEARN AN INSTRUMENT, LEARN HOW TO DANCE, DO MOVEMENT CLASSES. YOUR BODY IS YOUR INSTRUMENT! ALL ACTORS ARE DIFFERENT, FIND YOUR OWN WAY.

In a production of *Pinocchio* at the **Unicorn Theatre** in London, Eleanor played the Blue Fairy. Pantomimes are great opportunities for actors to find new ways of telling old favorite stories.

Blocking

The plan for where actors will stand and move to during the scene. It's figured out during rehearsals and is usually designed by the director so that the actors can be seen.

Hi, I'm Eleanor. I knew I wanted to act when I got jealous watching kids on TV. I did a summer theater course, and when I got my first role I stayed up all night because I was so excited. Later, I got to play a member of a girl band on a Nickelodeon TV series. Since then, I've gone to drama school, performed at stages around the UK, and started to write my own roles.

WHAT WOULD YOU DO IF YOU WEREN'T AN ACTOR?

If I wasn't an actor, I would love to be a set designer. I was really into art at school. For me, a big part of being an actor and a creative is being able to live in my imagination. What I loved about set design is that you'd create this whole intricate world.

WHAT DEGREES DO YOU HAVE?

I did Drama at high school, and then I auditioned for drama school. I went to the **Guildhall School of Music and Drama** in the UK, but there are lots of different ones you can apply to around the world. I then got a degree in Acting, which involved studying acting all day, every day. I loved it.

Pilot
The first episode of a television series. Sometimes, this will get made as a test before the full series gets approved for release.

HOW DO WRITING AND ACTING WORK TOGETHER?

I've written two pilot TV episodes with a writing partner who was very experienced in television. Even though I didn't start writing until I was thirty, I realized that I'd read so many scripts since I began acting at fifteen, that actually I did know how to do it. Since then, it's been flowing out.

ERYCK BRAHMANIA

DANCER

Eryck grew up in Essex, UK, and attended the Royal Ballet School in London from age eleven to nineteen. During that time, he worked with the Birmingham Royal Ballet. After graduating, he danced with the Hong Kong Ballet, the Rambert Dance Company, and Michael Clark Dance.

"When I was working for **Rambert Dance Company** at Sadlers Wells Theatre, London, my dad came to see me dance. He had never come before, even when I was a kid. That show was really special for me."

Hi, I'm Eryck. When I was in primary school, my mom sent me to dance classes. She made me a deal: If I attended classes, I would get a toy now and then. When I was ten years old, I was accepted at the Royal Ballet School. I was often the only boy, so I didn't have anyone else to compare myself to. At school, my dancing had been a secret that not many people knew about.

WHAT WAS IT LIKE TRAINING AT THE ROYAL BALLET SCHOOL?

From the age of eleven, I was dancing solidly every day for many hours alongside my regular schooling. I trained mainly in ballet, but I learned many other dance disciplines, too. By the time I left the **Royal Ballet School** at age nineteen, I would be training in the studio from 8:30 a.m. until 6:45 p.m. That's an insane amount of swinging a leg!

Choreography
The process of planning out a sequence of movements in a dance.

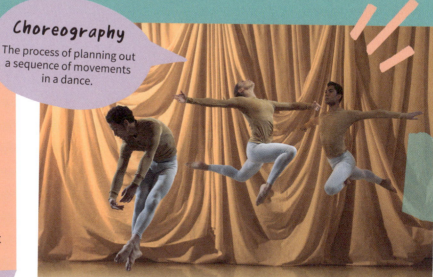

Contemporary Dance
A blend of elements from many dance styles that involves moving freely and fluidly.

WHAT SKILLS DOES A DANCER NEED TO HAVE?

If I were a dish, I think I'd be a chop suey—I'm very versatile! Dancers have to be able to pick up choreography quickly and learn to dance many different styles throughout their careers. The next challenge is making the movements your own, with your own unique styling and flavor that is brimming with your personality. Audiences can feel when someone is fully embodying the moves, as opposed to just doing the steps.

WHAT IS THE HARDEST PART ABOUT BEING A DANCER?

It can be a short career. You could get injured at any moment, which would mean you couldn't be involved in a project. You need to work hard to keep your body in the best shape. However, nowadays, dancers can branch out into many other avenues of dance like choreographing, movement direction, acting, and teaching. There's a load of options!

TO GET UP EVERY DAY AND DO THE THING THAT YOU LOVE IS A BLESSING.

RAJIV KARIA

COMEDIAN AND PRODUCER

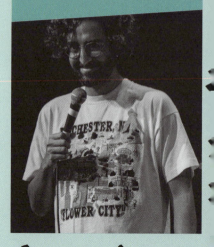

Rajiv Karia is a comedy writer, performer, and producer. He won the prestigious BBC Comedy Contract Writer Bursary in 2021 and has written material for TV and radio. He's produced UK Radio 4 episodes of The *Now Show*, *DM's Are Open*, and *Ken Cheng: Chinese Comedian* (which won a BBC Audio Drama Award).

Rajiv's solo stand-up hour *Gallivant* debuted at the **Edinburgh Fringe Festival** 2022 and transferred to London's **Soho Theatre**, before premiering on the UK's ITVX. The show asks the really important questions in life, like where can you find the best pizza outside of Naples. (The answer: **Dominoes**).

- PERFORMING ARTS -

Hey, I'm Rajiv. I always loved school plays and performing in general. When I got to college, I thought I'd keep doing plays, but after a few failed auditions, I set my sights elsewhere. The sketch comedy society had a very informal setup where anyone was welcome to come along. So I went along. Soon I realized that the comedy part of performance had always been my favorite bit. So I ditched the plays and kept the comedy. Then I just never stopped.

HOW WOULD YOU DESCRIBE YOUR STYLE ON STAGE?

Relaxed and conversational. I find the audience relaxes when the performer does. It means I can take my time with material and listen to what they like and don't like. I love using misdirection—which is when a comedian makes you think a joke is going in an obvious direction, but then they surprise you by taking it elsewhere.

WINNER

I'VE BEEN CHEATING AT SCRABBLE BY GRADUALLY LEARNING MORE WORDS MY ENTIRE LIFE!

Special
The best parts of a comedian's act that they have edited over the years—it's a big deal if your special gets recorded for a streaming site!

Skits Comedy
A series of short, amusing scenes, usually between one and ten minutes long. They're a great way to try out ideas with small groups of comedians.

HOW DID YOU DISCOVER YOUR LOVE OF COMEDY?

I had a primary school teacher who introduced me to writing skits. I don't know if I was more or less talented than everyone in our class, but I definitely enjoyed it the most. At college I studied law. It seemed like a good idea at the time, but pretty soon I realized I wasn't very interested in it. So I started looking around for something else to enjoy. I was lucky that there was a comedy scene at my college. I learned a lot there. Just not in the lecture halls.

WRITE AS MUCH AS YOU CAN. PERFORM AND SELF-PRODUCE AND PUT YOUR STUFF OUT THERE. IT'S ALWAYS BETTER TO HAVE MADE SOMETHING IMPERFECT RATHER THAN HOLDING SOMETHING BACK BECAUSE YOU'RE AFRAID IT WON'T BE PERFECT.

PHOTOGRAPHY

Every photographer is different in terms of what they capture and how they work: Some snap key moments in fast-moving events, others spend hours trying to create the perfect shot. Photographers work all across the creative spectrum: From independent artists, to producers of images for advertising and news outlets.

SKILLS

COMPOSITION

Photographers need to understand how to balance an image with different proportions of blank space and color.

TECH

Lens technologies and editing softwares change all the time, so a good photographer is always up to speed with the latest gadgets.

PEOPLE SKILLS

Photographers must connect with their subjects, often in a short amount of time. The best photos come when people are acting naturally.

EDIT

Digital photographers use editing software to alter their images and make them pop and communicate with an audience.

Most photos today are made by either:

1 imprinting an image onto film or

2 using a digital sensor to store an image as long strings of data.

But all photographers need to understand the basic techniques of how to capture an image.

ISO

A camera's light sensitivity. If the camera has a high ISO, it doesn't need lots of light from the outside world to get a good picture, but if there is lots of light, the shot can look grainy.

Shutter Speed

How quickly a photo is taken. A longer shutter speed will create a blurrier image across more time.

Aperture

The size of the opening in the camera lens. A large opening allows more light, giving a brighter photo.

COLIN LANE

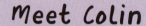

MUSIC AND STREET PHOTOGRAPHER

Colin Lane began his career as a music photographer touring with the rock band, The Strokes. His photographs capture once-in-a-lifetime moments and require him to pay close attention to what's happening around him. He has shot for other bands, including Kings of Leon and The National, and also worked in fashion photography, portraiture, and street photograph.

WATCH LOTS OF ALTERNATIVE MOVIES. YOU SHOULD ALWAYS BE EXPANDING YOUR VISUAL KNOWLEDGE, ESPECIALLY WHEN YOU'RE JUST STARTING OUT.

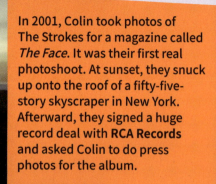

In 2001, Colin took photos of The Strokes for a magazine called *The Face*. It was their first real photoshoot. At sunset, they snuck up onto the roof of a fifty-five-story skyscraper in New York. Afterward, they signed a huge record deal with **RCA Records** and asked Colin to do press photos for the album.

Hey, I'm Colin. When I was thirteen or fourteen, I saw a movie called *Apocalypse Now* by a director named Francis Ford Coppola. It was a movie about the Vietnam War and man's descent into darkness. I may not have understood everything that was going on, but the images and cinematography made a big impression on me. From then on, I started to pay attention to the way movies looked. I thought to myself: "Maybe I want to do something visual."

WHAT ADVICE DO YOU HAVE FOR YOUNG PHOTOGRAPHERS?

Figure out what you like and concentrate on it. I shoot music, I shoot portraits, I shoot street, I shoot some fashion … that's just me. But it's worked against me throughout my career. Ad agencies and photo editors like it when you shoot one thing. They want to know exactly what they're going to get, and if you shoot too many things they become unsure. You should concentrate on one thing, at least at first. You can expand your repertoire later, after you've established yourself.

WHAT IS THE BEST THING ABOUT PHOTOGRAPHY?

Absolutely the best thing about my job is the feeling you get when you're shooting and the conditions are perfect—the light is perfect and everything is just going right, and you know you're getting some great images. And maybe something unexpected happens that makes it even better! When you're in that moment, it's such a rush.

HOW DO YOU CHOOSE WHICH PHOTOS TO USE?

If I have 3,000 images to look at, I'll try and do a quick first edit to cut that number in half. Then I may wait a day and do another edit, and keep trying to cut it in half until I have maybe 100 pictures. I can usually do that in three or four edits, depending on how many pictures I start with. I can't do it all at once: I need breaks so my mind isn't overwhelmed by pictures.

LUKE KIRWAN

STILLS PHOTOGRAPHER

Luke Kirwan is a photographer who captures still objects in striking ways. His photographs have been used in commercials for British Airways, Netflix, Adidas, Volkswagen, and John Lewis stores among many other incredible brands. His work is all about creating as much of the real image as possible in front of the camera rather than using CGI—though sometimes his photographs will make you do a double take!

IMAGE CREATION KEPT COMING OUT AS THE THING THAT BOUGHT ME THE MOST JOY.

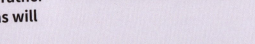

Luke worked with typographic designer Alan Kitching and set builder Mandy Smith on a commission for **Kia's** launch of its new model: the XCeed. Using balloons and Luke's editing magic, they created the illusion of a floating car.

Hey, I'm Luke. When I was young, my dad was a weekend wedding photographer, and when I became a teenager, he built a darkroom. I started taking pictures of my mates, and decided to do a night course in Photography at the London College of Communication. I saw an ad for a photographer's assistant, applied, and got the job. I was pretty clueless, but luckily the person I ended up working for understood that you have to start somewhere.

WHAT MAKES A GOOD PHOTOGRAPHER?

Single-mindedness and a good eye. You also have to be able to work well with other people and make them want to work with you again and again.

WHAT ARE THE BIGGEST CHALLENGES OF BEING A PHOTOGRAPHER?

If you want to be successful, it is all-consuming. It demands high levels of investment of your time and money (for equipment and transportation). And there is such a high level of competition in this industry. When you're getting work, the money can be very good, but you can't ever take it for granted.

WHO INSPIRES YOU?

I admire any photographer, artist, sculptor, filmmaker, or architect who has an identifiable style that they've crafted for themselves —rather than those who copy whatever feels contemporary at the time. Inspiration should come from all fields of creativity.

PRODUCT DESIGN

Being a successful product designer is all about understanding how people use the things in their life—whether that's a lemon squeezer, a kitchen table, or a backpack. It's a product designer's job to figure out what people want or need to make their lives easier, then designing products to make sure they look good, do their job well, and are safe and easy to use. If you can spot a problem and come up with a clever way to fix it, you're probably on to a good product design.

SKILLS

PROBLEM-SOLVING

Great product ideas come from spotting a problem with how something works and knowing how to fill the gap.

ENGINEERING

Product designers have to understand that all the different pieces of an object work together to create a working whole.

IDEA—TESTING

Product design requires lots of testing, in order to be sure that a design will work in lots of different scenarios.

PEOPLE - WATCHING

Good designers closely observe how people interact with a product, in case they use it differently from how the designer was expecting!

Look around the space you're in. What objects draw your attention? Just about every object in your home—however simple—was designed by someone. Someone chose the shape and materials for that lamp over there; someone else created the design for that mug of tea.
Take the chair you're sitting in. Is it designed to help you sit up straight or lean back and be cozy? Is it easy to fold up and put away, or is it more of a permanent fixture in the room? Different products are designed to solve different needs.

ANTONY JOSEPH

PRODUCT DESIGNER

Meet Antony

Antony Joseph is a product designer who owns the company Joseph Joseph with his twin brother, Richard. Whenever they create a product, they start by identifying an everyday problem. They make products that work beautifully and are designed to last a long time.

This laundry basket was designed to solve the problem of needing to separate different types of clothes for different washes! No more messy piles of lights and darks all over the floor. Genius!

THE ABILITY TO POINT TO SOMETHING AND SAY I DESIGNED THAT CAN BE A SOURCE OF GREAT PRIDE AND FULFILLMENT.

WHAT MAKES A GOOD PRODUCT DESIGNER / MAKER ?

Product design often involves finding creative solutions to complex problems. A good maker understands materials. They should also get to know processes for modeling and prototyping, so that they can test and improve their ideas. Access to a well-equipped workshop also helps.

Hi, I'm Antony. Because I'm dyslexic, lots of subjects were difficult for me at school, but I always loved art and drawing. When I designed a folding chair for one of my exams, I knew I'd found my passion. The first product I made with my company was a glass chopping board. Today, our products sell around the world and have won many design awards.

WHAT DEGREES DO YOU HAVE?

I went to art college and did a foundation course for a year, where I tried everything from photography to printmaking and sculpture. During my time there, I decided that product design was my favorite discipline and proceeded to study this at degree level.

Visability

How quickly someone can get going with your product. If it takes a long time to figure it out, it might need more fine-tuning!

Prototype

An initial model of something, usually created for testing and demonstration purposes.

Iterate

To improve a product or idea through review and redesign. It's how you get to the best solutions!

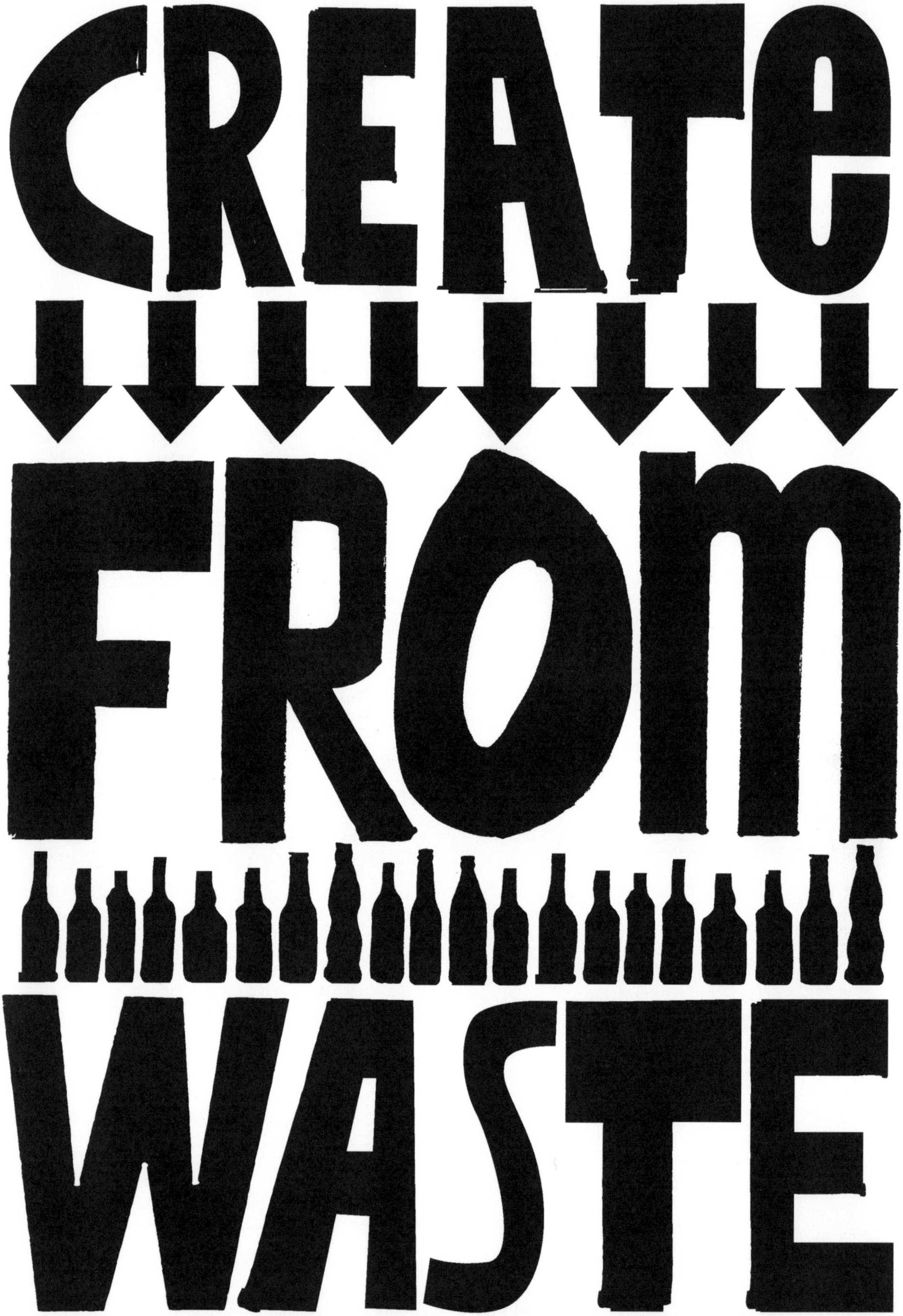
CREATE
FROM
WASTE

NADEEM DANIEL

CREATIVE DIRECTOR

Nadeem Daniel is a cofounder of Are You Mad, a design studio that transforms trash into treasure. His studio takes waste materials and recycles them into objects and furniture, meaning that their design practices are sustainable and also benefit the community. They break down products into their simplest states and work with creatives to imagine what else they might become.

HOW DO YOU HELP BRANDS?

We train and teach brands about how to turn their waste into a commodity. My role is to develop long-term relationships with them to make real change. Recently, we worked with Selfridges stores to create a bunch of custom retail display units for the showroom of their new program, Reselfridges: A resale, rental, repair, and recycle ecosystem for clothes. We cleaned and processed a ton of filthy plastic and turned it into displays that Dior bags can sit on.

ARE YOU MAD

Nad's company hired fifteen creative young people to collect waste from businesses around Carnaby Street in London. In forty days, they had collected 1.65 tons of plastic—that's 3,306 pounds! They then completely refitted their shop front exclusively using the plastic that they had recycled.

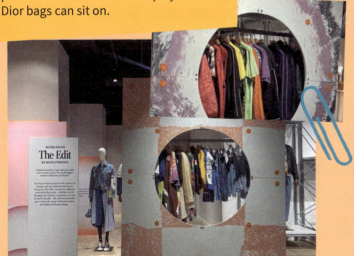

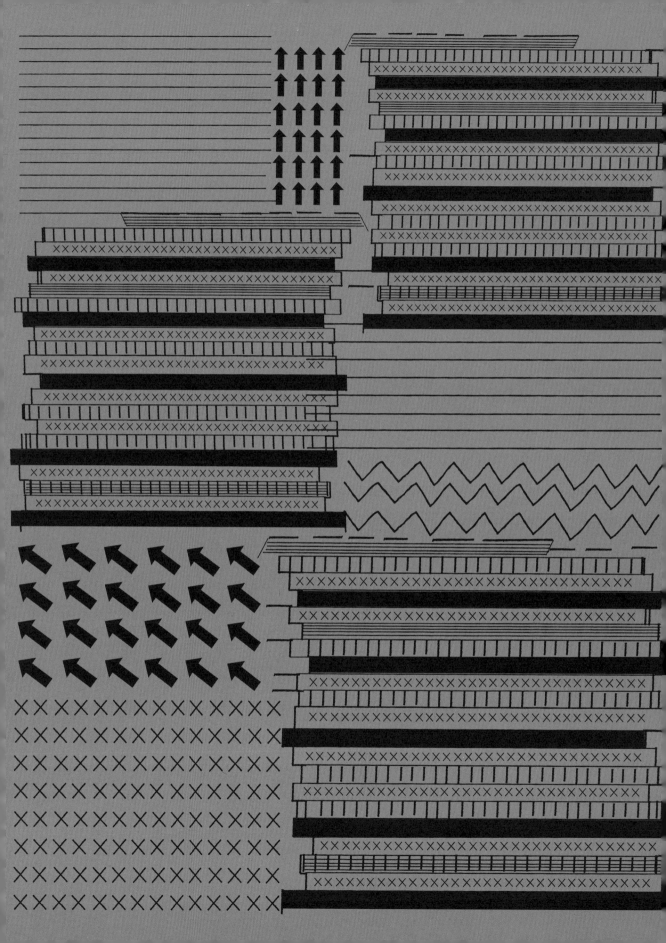

PUBLISHING

Publishing is a really broad industry, spanning books, magazines, newspapers, and all kinds of online publications. It's all about the process of writing, creating, and sharing content—such as stories, articles, or artwork—with an audience. It's an exciting way to express yourself and get your opinions heard and seen. The exciting thing is that it's become easier than ever to publish your own work, whether that's through print or digital platforms. A good place to start is by jotting down ideas or journaling, maybe starting a blog.

SKILLS

PRECISION

In publishing, words matter. Each word has a precise meaning—joyful is different from happy, peaceful is different to calm. Be specific!

INVENTIVENESS

Being original with text is vital. Can you think of a new or unique way to express something that people may have heard before?

TARGET AUDIENCE

When you write something, can you think about how it will be felt or understood by someone? You have to connect with your readers.

FOCUS

It takes a lot of attention to get a story just right. You have to be able to stick with an idea and see it through to the end.

==It's easy to start writing, just pick up a pen! Don't worry too much about getting the words right the first time==—the most important thing is to get your story down, whether it's a fantasy story or a description of something that happened in your day. Once you get to the end, you can go back and look at the sentences you wrote. Do they flow like music? Are the words specific enough to paint a vivid picture? Good writers also have to be good editors and tweak their work over and over to get it just right.

AJA BARBER

WRITER

Aja Barber's work as a writer focuses on sustainability and fashion. She likes to ask questions like, "Can we make and sell clothing in a way that's better for our planet?" She writes for many publications, from blogs to international newspapers and magazines, and has written a book titled *Consumed*!

Aja's book *Consumed: The Need for Collective Change* looks at how we make clothes, and how we can make them in a way that is better for the planet and the people who produce them.

CONSUMED
THE NEED FOR COLLECTIVE CHANGE:
COLONIALISM, CLIMATE CHANGE & CONSUMERISM

FUN FACT

The cover of *Consumed* was designed by RUDE Studios— the makers of the book in your very hands. See, we told you— graphics are everywhere!

Hey, I'm Aja. I cannot do maths to save my life. But I realized at a young age that I could write. I always enjoyed it. I also remember the first day my mother allowed me to pick out my own clothes. I was SO proud of myself. (And the outfit I picked!) If someone had told me that I would one day be writing books about the fashion industry and sustainability, I would have shouted "You're ridiculous!" But I'm doing it!

WHAT'S THE HARDEST THING ABOUT YOUR JOB?

The worst thing is having to use social media to constantly promote what you do. It's absolutely draining—especially if those platforms aren't paying you. It's like a job on top of a job. Recently, I started doing less public social media because it wasn't good for my mental health.

Sustainability

A social goal for people to coexist on Earth over a long time. The way that businesses work and people live can all be more oriented toward long-term health.

WHAT ARE YOUR TIPS FOR YOUNG WRITERS?

Learn as much as you possibly can about the area you want to be in.

 Find a unique angle; be a unique voice.

Even though we should all spend less time on the internet, it can be used to allow your voice to be heard.

Saying stuff that needs to be heard, but that no one else is saying yet, can be a doorway into the spaces you'd like to be in.

WHY DID YOU START WRITING ABOUT FASHION?

I love clothing. I want to know how it's made and I want to understand techniques. As a child, I went through so many phases of making things. Pressed flower cards, potholders, knitting, soapmaking, sewing. I also volunteered in a thrift store, and I began to understand how much clothing is being bought and discarded. This was eye-opening!

THE WORLD IS CHANGING SO RAPIDLY RIGHT NOW. THE JOB YOU MAY HAVE IN THE FUTURE MIGHT NOT EVEN EXIST TODAY!

FIONA LUMBERS

AUTHOR & ILLUSTRATOR

Fiona Lumbers writes and illustrates books for kids, including the very popular *Luna Loves* series. Her latest book, *Grandpa's Gift*, is about magical grandfathers and the beauty in everyday things. She also works on the BBC's 500 Words competition, illustrating stories written by kids like you!

Luna Loves is a series of books that Fiona created with British Children's Laureate Joseph Coelho, which is all about exploring new activities, bonding with family, and learning lessons when things go wrong.

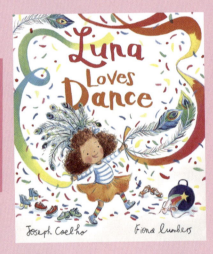

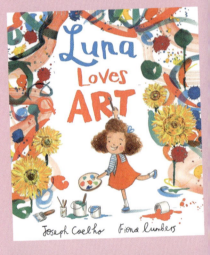

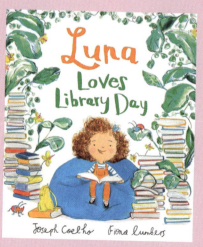

Hi, I'm Fiona. I always loved art lessons at school, and for as long as I can remember, I dreamed of going to art college and pursuing a career in the arts. Initially, I thought that I wanted to study fashion, but that all changed when I discovered how much I loved painting and printmaking on my Art Foundation course. I fell in love with the freedom to experiment!

KEEP EXPERIMENTING. KEEP A SKETCHBOOK HANDY AT ALL TIMES. NOTICE THE WORLD AROUND YOU, AND LET IT INFORM YOUR WORK. FIND WHAT MAKES YOU HAPPY, AND KEEP DOING THAT.

WAS IT DIFFICULT TO BECOME A CHILDREN'S BOOK AUTHOR AND ILLUSTRATOR?

My route into illustrating was not very linear, but I feel that everything that came before it has informed the work I make now. Before my current career, I exhibited my paintings, worked as a visiting lecturer, and taught art in prisons for a number of years. I think I've always told stories through the art I make, and this is just another way of doing that.

WHAT'S THE BEST THING ABOUT YOUR JOB?

The best thing is that I get to make stories that can take readers on all kinds of journeys. It's a real privilege. I've met countless other authors and illustrators who have become great friends and colleagues. I've traveled all over the UK and further afield sharing stories, and I get to spend a large part of my time making art.

Folktale

A story, usually with a message, that has been passed down through many years from adults to children.

WHAT DO YOU THINK MAKES A GOOD CREATIVE MAKER?

Experimenting, pushing your work in different directions, trying new ways of making, being aware of current trends, but ultimately staying true to the type of work you want to make.

BOOKBINDING

Bookbinding probably began in India in the 2nd century BCE, where religious texts were etched onto palm leaves and bound together with twine between two boards. The boards protected the texts from sunlight, water stains, and other damage. Smart, huh?

It was a few more centuries before the Romans realized that binding pages into books would be so much better than long, annoying scrolls! But they did start making blank notebooks for personal writing, so anyone could record their thoughts and stories.

Tilly de Verteuil

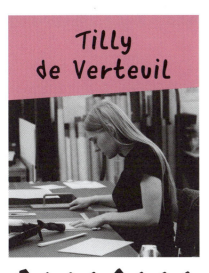

Tilly de Verteuil runs a small bookbinding press in southeast London called Tillman Press. She creates high-quality handcrafted books and boxes that combine artisanal craft and modern design processes. Her interest began when she wanted to publish her own book. She found that the process cost so much to have it the way she imagined, that she learned how to do it herself.

Tilly fell in love with the process, then got a job at a small bindery and print company to learn all that she could about making books.

She is interested in which materials other than paper can be bound into books. One project she is working on uses rice paper sheets, bound with water to make the sheets dissolve into each other as sugar. Now that's thinking outside the box!

TO BE A GOOD BOOKBINDER, YOU NEED TO BE CLEAN, PRECISE, AND PATIENT. I WASN'T NATURALLY ANY OF THESE THINGS, WHICH WAS EXACTLY WHY I WANTED TO LEARN.

LEAH BOULTON

MANAGING EDITOR

Leah Boulton works at Vintage, an imprint of Penguin Random House publishing. She spends her days shaping manuscripts as they come through the publishing process, right up until they're ready to hit print! Her job involves copy editing and proofreading books, which lets her do lots of reading and playing around with language.

Leah worked on *How to Build a Boat* by Elaine Feeney, a story about a boy who changes the lives of his teachers. The book was longlisted for the 2023 Booker Prize—one of the most important awards in the publishing world.

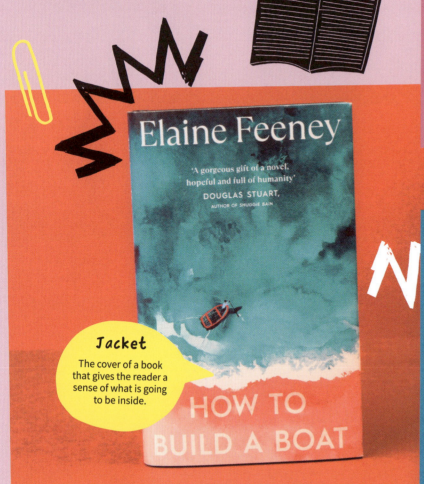

Jacket

The cover of a book that gives the reader a sense of what is going to be inside.

WHAT MAKES A GOOD MANAGING EDITOR?

A good Managing Editor should be focused, precise, and able to communicate with various different teams across the business! Attention to detail is really important since we're the final gatekeepers of a manuscript before it hits the shelves, so we're responsible for catching those pesky typos that tend to slip into books! Flexibility and multitasking are also key—we work on various books at the same time, so you need to be able to shift from project to project.

Hi, I'm Leah, and I'm a total bibliophile (meaning I love books!). When I was a kid, my parents struggled to pull my head out of any book I was reading, so I knew I wanted to be part of the process of making them. I always had a knack for being observant, and I always found the process of rewording a particularly knotty phrase satisfying. I also loved writing—penning fun messages in a friend's birthday card and sending postcards to my grandma.

WHAT'S THE BEST THING ABOUT BEING AN EDITOR?

The best thing is being paid to lose yourself in a story—be it a historical drama, a nonfiction book about the hidden properties of fungi, or even a comic book! It's a pleasure to be let into the world the author has created and help them on their journey. The range of content that comes across our desks is huge, so I'm constantly learning new things and reading stories from fresh perspectives.

Manuscript

The text of a book, worked on by authors and editors, before it is published.

Imprint

A group within a larger publishing company that focuses on particular genres or themes. You can see the imprint on the spine of the book!

IF YOU WEREN'T AN EDITOR, WHAT WOULD YOU BE?

One part of my job is proofreading all our book covers—they're beautifully designed and can really help make a book stand out on the shelves. If I didn't do editing (and had the artistic talent!), I'd love to be a jacket designer and help bring an author's words to life with an iconic cover image.

SURROUND YOURSELF WITH BOOKS!

FIGURE OUT WHAT YOUR FAVORITE STYLE OF WRITING IS, BUT ALSO TRY TO READ THINGS OUT OF YOUR COMFORT ZONE TO LEARN WHAT DIFFERENT KINDS OF READERS LIKE.

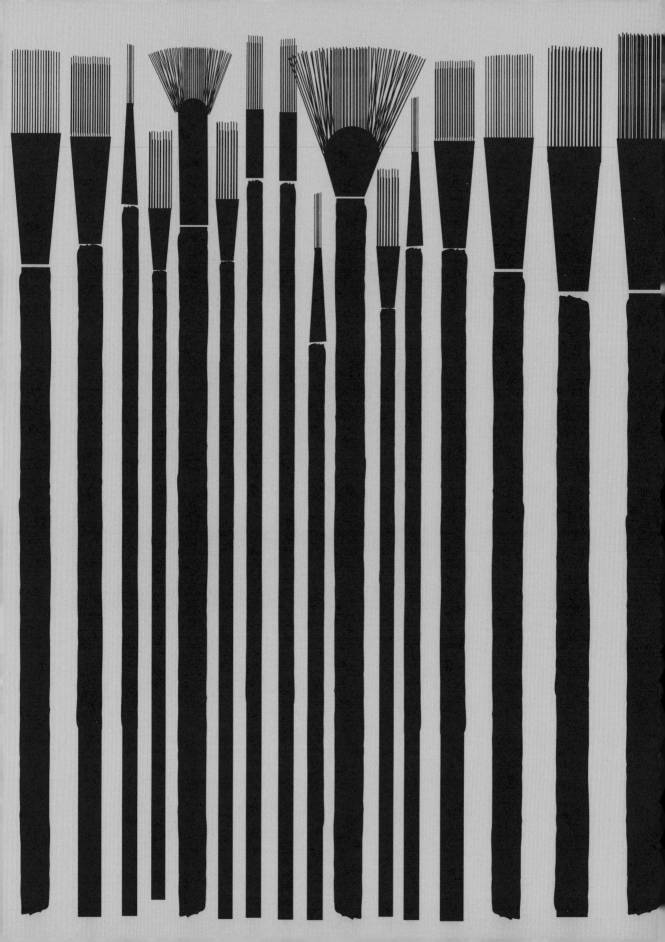

VISUAL ARTS

////////////////////////////////////

There are many different forms of visual arts: Painting, printmaking, sculpting—really any visual tool that you might feel drawn to in order to express yourself! Some artists choose to focus on one specific medium like murals or graffiti, while others mix and match many different forms to create new ways of expressing themselves. Visual arts are important because they help people share ideas and offer different viewpoints. You're creating something that other people can see, feel, and enjoy.

skills

COLORS

Do you have an eye for which shades go well together? Think about how to create colors by mixing different shades together.

TEXTURES

Artists work with different materials —soft or hard, smooth or stubbly—to create a particular mood or feeling.

EXPERIMENTATION

It's important for artists to be experimental. Creating a new perspective may well involve trying new techniques to see what works best.

DEDICATION

Creating art takes time and effort. It's important to be able to stay focused and work through challenges or setbacks.

The arts have been around for thousands of years. Since ancient times, people have made drawings, masks, and sculptures to tell stories and express their feelings. And throughout human history, there have been different movements in art, as people try to express new ideas and make sense of the changing world we live in. Different cultures also produce different types of art. Many of the most famous artworks throughout history can be seen in museums around the world, which are open for anyone to visit! Try to learn about all of the different artistic traditions, and see which ones inspire you!

BROKEN FINGAZ

FINGAZ STUDIO
PEACE IN THE MIDDLE EAST

MULTIDISCIPLINARY ARTIST

Meet Unga

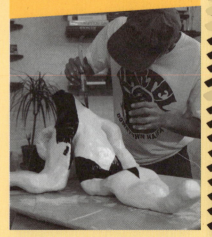

Unga is a member of Broken Fingaz Collective, a group of artists based in Israel who work together on projects. It began at school, with four friends who started creating art together—and now they have members all over the world. For twenty years, they worked together as a graffiti crew and have expanded their work to include painting, design, animation, sculpture, and installation.

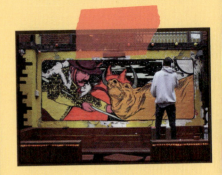

In 2022, Broken Fingaz painted a giant mural—*Bird*—as a commission for a street art festival in Belgium. Afterward, they released a print of their image and donated their proceeds to refugees from Ukraine.

Hi, I'm Unga, and I paint giant murals. Well, actually, I do lots of different types of art—I make posters, ceramics, and art prints. When I was a kid, I loved drawing and learned to use tools like Photoshop. My friends and I started organizing parties that combined graffiti and music, and we would design posters to promote our events. When people saw our posters, they started asking us if we could design for them.

WHILE STARTING OUT, IT'S OKAY TO DRAW INSPIRATION FROM OTHER ARTISTS, BUT IT'S CRUCIAL TO DEVELOP AND EVOLVE YOUR OWN UNIQUE STYLE!

HOW WOULD YOU DESCRIBE YOUR STYLE?

Broken Fingaz art is very colorful and often has lots of different characters and shapes. We use our art to send messages about important issues, like the environment or social justice. We also like to mix different styles of art and culture, so our art might have influences from different countries or time periods.

HOW DID YOU DEVELOP YOUR STYLE?

Practice! We were drawing and painting all the time, thinking about different styles and opening our minds to inspiration. Also, because our art is so public and it's up on walls, people will see it and give us feedback, which helps us change and refine.

DID IT TAKE A LONG TIME TO GET NOTICED?

It took ten years to get mural commissions but during this time we got skilled at making things. The turning point in our journey came when a friend from the embassy in Beijing commissioned us to create a large mural at an art fair. This opportunity challenged us to step up our game and work together as a team of four artists.

Limited Edition

These are artworks or prints that are made in small groups and might become more valuable because they are less common.

WE NEED CREATIVITY MORE THAN EVER

UNLEASH YOUR CREATIVE SUPER POWERS

FLO PERRY

PAINTER, WRITER & ILLUSTRATOR

Flo Perry is a portrait artist who paints people and their pets. For many years, she worked as a cartoonist and writer at Buzzfeed internet site. She has since written her own book and illustrated several for other people.

THE ONLY THING THAT YOU DEFINITELY HAVE TO BE GOOD AT TO BE AN ARTIST IS JUST THE DOING OF IT. I MEAN THE LITERAL GETTING THE PAINTS OUT, OR THE TABLET, OR YOUR INSTRUMENT, OR YOUR CAMERA, AND DOING YOUR ART. PRACTICE AS MUCH AS POSSIBLE.

Flo is often busy painting commissions of pet portraits, like this one of her own cat, Crisp. "It feels nice when important art people choose your work to be in important exhibitions," she says, "but it feels just as nice when people choose you to paint their pet out of all the many artists out there."

- VISUAL ARTS -

Hi, I'm Flo. When I was three, I wanted to be a fashion designer, but then when I was twelve, I decided I wanted a normal job where you had a boss and got paid the same amount every month. I tried that, but it was too boring, so I quit. I started doing painting in my spare time again when I was about twenty-four. I put my paintings online, and more and more people wanted them.

HOW HAS YOUR CAREER DEVELOPED OVER TIME?

I did a Chemistry degree, which has been 0% useful in my adult career, but it gave me the time to get into student journalism. After college, I worked for BuzzFeed as a writer, and they encouraged me to start illustrating my online articles. I was into doing cartoon illustrations to make people laugh. But now, I'm much more interested in doing more realistic paintings that are very special to the people who commission them.

Commission
A piece of artwork (often one of a kind) that is created for a particular customer.

WHAT DOES YOUR AVERAGE DAY LOOK LIKE?

9:30 AM	My girlfriend leaves for work. Procrastinate for at least 30 minutes.
10:00 AM	Think, "OMG, I should have started work half an hour ago" and reply to some emails.
10:15 AM	Paint until lunchtime.
12:00 AM	Go for a swim.
1:00 PM	Paint some more.
4:00 PM	Watch TV and eat chocolate buttons on the sofa.

SAL VELLUTO

COMIC-BOOK ARTIST

Sal Velluto is a comic book artist born and raised in Italy and now living in the USA. He has worked on hundreds of comics including Marvel's *Black Panther* and *Moon Knight*, and DC's *Justice League*. Previously, he worked in animation, producing Saturday Morning Cartoons. Sal also drew the storyboards and layouts for shows like *Spiderman and His Amazing Friends*, *Transformers*, and *The Incredible Hulk*.

Sal became the most prolific artist on **Marvel's** *Black Panther* comic. The Black Panther is the first black superhero in American comics. In 2018, **Marvel** made a very successful movie based on the comic, starring the actor Chadwick Boseman. Some scenes of the movie and some details of *Black Panther's* costumes were inspired by Sal's drawings.

A GOOD COMIC-BOOK ARTIST NOT ONLY KNOWS HOW TO DRAW (NO MATTER THE STYLE) BUT KNOWS HOW TO TELL A STORY WITH PICTURES.

Hi, I'm Sal. As a nine-year-old, I used to draw a four-page comic book that had the kids in my neighborhood as heroes and villains (depending on how friendly they were to me). I would sell copies for money or snacks. When I was twelve, I submitted a fan drawing to the Italian *Batman* magazine, and they published it! I decided then that I wanted to draw comics when I grew up.

ANY TIPS FOR ASPIRING COMIC-BOOK ARTISTS?

They're the same tips you would give someone for becoming a soccer player. If you want to play in the big leagues, you have to bring yourself to the same level as the players of that league. It doesn't matter how long or how much work it takes. Preparation is the key. I was most successful in life when the opportunities presented themselves, and I was prepared to face them.

WHAT MAKES A GOOD COMIC BOOK ARTIST?

You can tell a comic book artist is good when you look at a page without reading the words, and you can still tell what's going on. That's called good Visual Storytelling. You can be a great artist, but if your pictures don't tell a story, comic books are not for you.

IT TAKES MANY ARTISTS TO ILLUSTRATE A COMIC BOOK:

Inker
draws with ink, or a tablet, over the pencil drawings to make the art reproducible in print.

Colorist
colors the story, usually on a computer.

Panel
an individual frame or single drawing in the sequence of a comic book.

Penciller
Draws the story with pencil on a large piece of paper or on a tablet.

...and MORE!

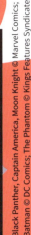

ACKNOWLEDGEMENTS

This book was brought to you by—you guessed it!—creatives! We would like to give a hearty THANK YOU to all of the unbelievable mentors featured in these pages. Your wisdom and generosity inspired us every day that we worked on this project. Additionally, to all of the incredible photographers and image creators who graciously allowed us to use their work—thank you for joining in our mission.

If you're a kid, and you're still reading this, remember: It's JUST as important to document your work as it is to make it in the first place. Show off your stuff!

To Sabrina Bisi, the brilliant, tireless designer behind these pages: Your approach to each feature sparkles with care and deep thoughtfulness. You have made this book a triumph. And a big thank you as well to Rebecca Fallon for writing and editing the words in this book and helping to develop our punchy, inspired voice. To Mary Hurd, for kicking this project off and getting our first interviews off the ground: You made it all feel possible. Talk about collaboration, huh?

A massive thanks to our creative business sponsors—B+A Reps, Bic, Caroline Gardener, Everyone Agency, Noam, and Ustwo—who boosted our initial fundraising and provided invaluable support along the way. Special thanks to the brilliant Shelley Nicoli and Leah James at the Laurence King imprint of Hachette Children's, who published this version of the book with care and patience, making it accessible to many.

CREDITS

Introduction © Rude Studio Ltd; **Antoinette Nassopoulos Erickson** / All images © Foster + Partners; **Jianfei Chu** / All images © Zaha Hadid Architects; **Alex Shipp** / All images courtesy of Meristem; **Matt Jones** / Nike Store image © Accept & Proceed / Basketball Court © Nike / Rastko Šurdić; Burger King © ; **Karen Martin** / Burger King image © Lou Escobar / Tesco; **Raoul Shah** / Red Smiley Faces by Timothy Curtis / Black and White Break Dancers courtesy of Janette Beckman / Cartoon Paint Drops by HuskMitNavn; **Dave Rax** / All images © Dave Rax & Koto Studio; **Franki Goodwin** / All images courtesy of Saatchi & Saatchi and Franki&Jonny; **Jill Molyneux** / Jack and the Beanstalk, courtesy of Oxford Playhouse / Robots (Puppit + Digit), photo by Tom Walsh courtesy of Polymath Pictures, commissioned by Applause / Dick Whittington costume © TAGLIVE; **Katrina Lindsey**; **Jack Baxter** / Alexis Michelle in blueberry couture, as featured in Season 8 of RuPaul's Drag Race: All Stars, photo © Kat Hennessey; **Nam Tran** / Headshot by Tom Silvester / Bahamut, Photos by Valerie Bernardini; **Laura Smith** / Studio shots by Jesse Wild; **Rose Stallard** / Portrait by Grainne Quinlan / Working on Time and Space, Photo by Grainne Quinlan / Mugs designed by Rose Stallard from the Richard Brendon X Print Club London Collection; **Dines** / All images courtesy of Dines; **Kodj Glover** / Headshot by Jake Ranford for FootPatrol / Workshop photos by Paolo Rizzi for ustwo; **Harry Witham** / River Medway photo © Tom Buck Photography / Jack Baxter in Pink Jacket and Jumpsuit / Jack Baxter in Glasses and Blue Dress / Jack Baxter in Custom Red Ball gown / Cheryl Hole photo © Matty Parks @mtyparks 6. Exhibition photos © Martin Turner; **Asya Smailbegovic**/ ASOS images © ASOS.com Limited; **Garth Jennings** / Stills from Sing and Sing 2 © Universal Studios / Son of Rambow © Paramount Pictures; **Jonny Moore** / Doctor Strange Statue (assistants: Gavin Fulcher and Christianne Barbknecht); **Erica McEwan** / All concept drawings © Painting Practice / His Dark Materials film stills © Bad Wolf / San Junipero, Black Mirror / Rolo Haynes Black Museum, Black Mirror / USS Callister, Black Mirror © Netflix; **Pips Taylor** / Photos by Adiam Photography / Pips and Nile Rodgers, photo by Robin Boot; **Thomasina Smith** / All images courtesy of Thomasina Smith / Headshot by Patti West; **Mike Skrgatic** / Lizard, Butterfly, Seahorse © Sky Creative / Honda Dream Makers Campaign, courtesy of Time Based Arts, Wieden + Kennedy, and Honda Motor Europe Ltd / Three Mobile: Phone History Campaign: Snake Selfie featuring Abigail O Wilson / Biblical masses featuring Elroy Powell / Channel 4 Idents; **Danny Gray** / Photos courtesy of ustwo games; **May Villani** / Farm Heroes Saga © King Animals and tea cup © Pujee&Bujee 358; **Abi and Rupert Meats** / All images © Rude Studio Limited; **Ocki Magill** / All photos courtesy of Blue Shop Cottage; **Sayantan Mukhopadhyay** / Installation view, Christo and Jeanne-Claude: Boundless © Matt Chung, 2023, Image courtesy of Saatchi Gallery, London; **Chelsea-Louise Berlin** / Installation view, SWEET HARMONY: RAVE | TODAY © Justin Piperger, 2019 Image courtesy of the Saatchi Gallery, London / Rave flyers from the Berlin collection, first reproduced in the book Rave Art by Chelsea-Louise Berlin / Installation view, Beyond the Streets London © 2023 Image courtesy of Saatchi Gallery, London / Installation view, Beyond the Streets London © Matt Chung, 2023 Image courtesy of Saatchi Gallery, London; **Bicep** / Bicep Headshot © Dan Medhurst / Bicep on stage with multi-colour swirl background © Antonio Pagano / Andy and Matt with Blue Background © Sam Mulvey / Bicep on stage with fire background © Antonio Pagano / Bicep on stage with water background © Dan Medhurst / Bicep on stage with blue maze at Brixton Academy © Khris Cowley, courtesy of Ninja Tune / Bicep on stage with red geometry at Zeal © Luke Dyson / Digital hands artwork © Zak Norman / Bicep mixing with red background © Sam Mulvey / Technicolor synthesiser © Zak Norman / Bicep Album Art courtesy of Ninja Tune / Isles design by Studio Degrau / Bicep design by Royal Studio; **Rae Morris** / Photo by Rueben Bastian Lewis / Rae Backstage, Photo by Callum Mills / Rae's Notebooks, Photo by Leo Goddard / Rae at the Piano, Photo by Rueben Bastian Lewis / Rae On Stage, Photo by JP Boardman; **Nigel Adams** / Pale Blue Eyes, photo by Sophie Jouvenaar / Hassle Records Logo © Hassle Records / Full Time Hobby Logo © Full Time Hobby / Brutus Recording Session, photo by Eva Vlonk / Brutus Vinyl Album and Stickers, photo for Dinked / Casey recording at Middle Farm, photo by Martyna Bannister / Casey sitting on the floor, photo by Martyna Bannister / Dana Gavanski, photo by Kirico Ueda / Last of the Great Thunderstorm Warnings by The Besnard Lakes, 2021. Art by DLT, exclusive edition for Dinked / Brutus Performance, photo by Robin Goossens; **Naomi Larsson Piñeda** / Naomi at the Moth Club, Photos by Jon Clements / Naomi Headshots, Photos by Chris Patmore; **Eleanor Wyld** / Pinnocchio, The Unicorn Theatre © Ellie Kurttz / Eleanor Wyld and Seyan Sarvan in The Boys are Kissing: Photo by Danny Kaan @dannywithacamera / Eleanor Wyld, Philip Correia, Amy McAllister and Seyan Sarvan in The Boys are Kissing: Photo by Danny Kaan @dannywithacamera / Eleanor Wyld in Leopoldstadt: Photo by Marc Brenner / Headshot, Photo by Frank Burke / Still of Eleanor Wyld in OXV: The Manual, © Darren Paul Fisher / The Merchant of Venice, The Globe, © Tristram Kenton; **Eryck Brahmania** / One arm flip, photo by Hugo Glendinning / Headshot, photo by Karen Yeomans / Eryck in Carmen at Queen Elizabeth Hall in front of sofa, photos by Andrej Uspenski / Eryck in Carmen at Queen Elizabeth Hall on sofa, photo by Annabel Moeller / Dancing in red costume, photos by Grace Kathryn Landefeld / Eryck in Carmen at Queen Elizabeth Hall, with Natalia Osipova in red hat, George Marinakis / Eryck in Carmen at Queen Elizabeth Hall, high angle photo, George Marinakis / Photo by Chris Nash; **Rajiv Karia** / Orange Suit, Photo by Matt Stronge / Rajiv and Olga at 21 Soho, courtesy of 21 Soho / Performance photos by Ed Moore; **Antony Joseph** / All images © Joseph Joseph; **Nadeem Daniel** / All images courtesy of Are You Mad; **Colin Lane** / Colin with The Strokes, photo by Zander Lane; **Luke Kirwan** / Yellow car with balloons © Kia / Silver car with automated broom © Volkswagen; **Aja Barber** / Book Launch Photos © Stephen Cunningsworth / Headshots © Stephen Cunningsworth / Book Cover Design by Rude Studios; **Fiona Lumbers** / Luna Loves series and Ghost Orchid were published by Andersen Press / The Secret Sky Garden was published by Simon & Schuster / My Tree was published by Scholastic; **Tilly De Verteuil** / All images courtesy of Tilly De Verteuil; **Leah Boulton** / How to Build a Boat by Elaine Feeney / Jacket illustration © Lili Wood, Design © Suzanne Dean / The Wren, The Wren. © Anne Enright 2023; **Unga** / All images and Colouring Book Drawings © Broken Fingers Collective; **Flo Perry** / All images courtesy of Flo Perry; **Sal Velluto** / Black Panther, Captain America, Moon Knight © Marvel Comics / Batman © DC Comics / The Phantom © Kings Features Syndicate.